GET YOUR

A Five-Step Guide

CAREER

to Achieve the Success

IN SHAPE

You Need, Want, and Deserve

DR. CANDACE STEELE FLIPPIN

PRAISE FOR
GET YOUR CAREER IN SHAPE

"Dr. Candace Steele Flippin empowers women with a robust framework to challenge a glass ceiling system within their own minds. This book will change the shape of their career trajectory—and help readers reach that seemingly elusive career milestone."
—Tyree C. Daniels, executive chairman at Memphis College Preparatory

"A good dose of medicine to restore, recharge, and refocus on career success. Whether you are just starting your career, recently divorced, or living your best life, Dr. Candace Steele Flippin's personal story, potent advice, and practical tools should resonate with women at every stage of their life."
—Tabrina Davis, vice president of marketing and communication at Methodist Le Bonheur Healthcare

"A foundational framework for all women in the workforce. Hard work alone doesn't necessarily lead to career success. Women in all stages of their career will benefit from the guidance and perspective provided in *Get Your Career in SHAPE*."
—Jasmine Brett Stringer, professional speaker and award-winning author of **Seize Your Life: How to Carpe Diem Every Day**

"Dr. Candace Steele Flippin's valuable guide is full of insights and testimonials that my clients can relate to and learn from at any stage in their career. These research-based strategies will help shape the career you deserve with intention and success."
—Alison Battaglia, PhD, principal of Riso Empowerment Consulting

"A must-read for young professionals. Although it speaks more directly to female professionals, this book is helpful to anyone seeking different viewpoints for navigating a more multigenerational and multicultural workplace. The blend of the personal, professional, and academic perspective provides common-sense solutions for career advancement."

—*Gregg Lunceford, PhD, author of* **Exit from Work**, *retirement researcher, and leading financial planning expert*

"A true guide to earning the success that you have been working so hard for. Dr. Candace Steele Flippin encourages and educates women across all ages, experience levels, and socioeconomic backgrounds to perform and succeed in their chosen career paths. Filled with both research and anecdotal evidence, Dr. Candace Steele Flippin outlines the problems facing women in the workforce and how to overcome roadblocks to success. While acknowledging institutional impediments, Dr. Candace Steele Flippin also discusses how women can be their own worst enemies when it comes to starting and advancing their careers.

"It's time to break out of the rut and get access to the vision you have for your career. Whether you are just starting your career or have been at it for decades, Dr. Candace Steele Flippin's system makes career success attainable to anyone."

—*The Lost Chapter, LLC, bookstore*

"Finally, a practical guide that women can use to take ownership of their careers, learn from their challenges, and create a path to their success. *Get Your Career in SHAPE* is an absolute must-have for your professional library!"

—*Markita Jack, head of diversity, equity, and inclusion at Iterable*

ISBN-13: 978-1-63489-501-9

Library of Congress Catalog Number has been applied for.
Printed in the United States of America
First Printing: 2022

26 25 24 23 22   5 4 3 2 1

Cover design by Nupoor Gordon
Interior design by Dan Pitts

Wise Ink Creative Publishing
807 Broadway St NE
Suite 46
Minneapolis, MN 55413

ACKNOWLEDGMENTS

I thank my mentees Rachael, Tamika, and Kassidy, for pushing me to write this book, and Cindy for her challenge to scale my idea and message.

I am grateful for TEDx Memphis for its support in providing a platform for my research. A very special thanks to the late psychologist Dr. Albert Bandura and his research on self-efficacy, which set me on my journey as a scholar. Thank you to the Weatherhead School of Management at Case Western Reserve University for creating a community of engaged scholars focused on advancing the fields of management practice.

Get Your Career in SHAPE is the culmination of the work and efforts of a fantastic team. I am blessed to have people travel my journey with me—much love to Thomas, and my family, who motivate me and keep me grounded.

I am tremendously grateful to Dara and Roseanne, without whom this book would not exist. I am very appreciative of everyone who helped with the background research, development, editing, and support. Finally, I thank Abbie, Alison, Amanda, Charlette, Janine, Jeri, LaTarshia, Laurel, Hanna, Natasha, Renee, Stacy, Tami, Vicki, other editors and designers, and supporters for helping me get this book over the finish line.

*This book is dedicated to all women
who believe they need, want,
and deserve to achieve more from their careers.*

TABLE OF CONTENTS

Author's Note..1

Introduction...3

How to Apply the SHAPE Framework 12

Self-Efficacy Check Questionnaire 16

Getting to the Green Career Zone Behaviors 18

Chapter 1: Save your money so finances won't get in the way
of your career options 21

Chapter 2: Hard Work is subjective—make sure you and
your boss are aligned 41

Chapter 3: Advocate for yourself so you are not the one
holding your career back 61

Chapter 4: Persevere to navigate your career journey
over the long term 89

Chapter 5: Educate yourself on how to expand your skills
and knowledge throughout your career 113

Where to Go from Here 133

About the Study..137

Appendix 1: Self-efficacy assessment 139

Appendix 2: SHAPE action template 143

Appendix 3: Getting the most out of your support circle 149

About the Author 151

AUTHOR'S NOTE

The book you're about to read combines my research and career experiences as both a practitioner and a scholar. Just as you may rely on personal and professional resources to help with physical health at different stages of life, this book can help you build and tap into personal and professional resources to support the shape of your career. My goal is to give you a prescription for career success filled with practical, research-based insights and tools for your unique path no matter where you are in your career journey.

Some of you readers may have a treasure trove of supporters and advisors. Or you may be making your way through your career with limited or no assistance. The point of this book is to help and support you along your journey.

Many of the tools I offer here will resonate and get you excited for the future. Others will require you to put the book down for a moment and really reflect on your own goals, challenges, strengths, and weaknesses. It's all good. The key is to keep going.

As you read this book, reflect on how to apply it to your own life, and remember that the choices are all yours. Through every step, you choose to make decisions on how you want to progress. Be sure to engage your support systems (e.g., friends, family, mentors, support circles, etc.) and share the book's concepts with others to reinforce and encourage your journey. I'm here to help guide you to the best choices for you.

INTRODUCTION

"I would say the worst advice is to be told I can't do something or achieve a goal I want."

—Anne, Gen X, accountant

self-efficacy

noun [U] • PSYCHOLOGY • specialized

a person's belief that they can be successful when carrying out a particular task

Source: *Cambridge Advanced Learner's Dictionary & Thesaurus,* Cambridge University Press.

One thing I love about my professional journey is getting to speak with and learn from women in all sorts of career stages of their own. Some of the women I meet are just beginning their careers, others are midcareer, some are unsure of what to do next, and some are at the top of their game. While I'm often called on for advice, I find that I grow from the experience.

Sometimes these women see my titles and positions (C-suite executive, doctor, author, speaker, board member, etc.) and say to me, "Candace, you have to tell me your secret. I would love to be where you are, but I just don't have enough [fill in the blank—experience, education, skill, etc.]." They have so many amazing stories, skills, and insights. However, as they share their backgrounds, it becomes clear that their level of self-efficacy—the vital ingredient needed to translate their goals into career movement—is holding them back. I get it. Women often question our skills and abilities, believing we don't have enough experience or the right qualifications. Men typically don't think this way. They usually believe they are qualified, even when they aren't.[1]

As a communications executive and multigenerational workplace scholar, I'm often asked about my career journey. I suspect it's tempting to look at me and assume my career was a straight line—a series of boxes I checked to achieve success. As you will learn reading this book, this was not the case.

When people ask me how I have achieved career success, I tell them that my three most important focus factors for my future are resilience, perspective, and hope. I believe we need all three to succeed. There has been no better time to focus on these tenets than now.

At the time of this introduction, we are finally approaching cautious optimism about the end of a pandemic that has raged for over a year and a half. We have recently lived through a resurgence of the issue of race in America, with police brutality and other tragedies reigniting flames across the country. Communities are all on the verge of stepping into the "new normal." No matter where people are in their careers, as we navigate the COVID-19 pandemic there seems to be a collective sense of stopping to catch our breaths and take stock of where we are and what we want to achieve. We now want to focus on the things that really matter.

---

1 Mohr, T. S. (2014). *Why women don't apply for jobs unless they're 100% qualified.* Harvard Business Review. https://hbr.org/2014/08/why-women-dont-apply-for-jobs-unless-theyre-100-qualified

So many people are taking this time of global "pause" to share their stories.

Here is mine.

It's ironic that the foundational acronym for my career framework is SHAPE, because to be totally honest, my professional life hasn't always been "in SHAPE" at all. In fact, there have been several times in my career where I felt uncertain, frustrated, and alone. However, as an optimist, I believed deeply that I could get on track to help myself and others.

Many of you reading this book may have seen my TEDx Talk: "Are You Talking to Me? What Women Really Want . . . at Work," sponsored by TEDxMemphis, where I introduced the save, hard work, advocate, persevere, and educate concepts. But for those who haven't, here's what happened to set me on this ambitious journey to transform workplaces.

Back in 2013, I went to graduate school to earn my doctorate in management. This educational investment came after over fifteen years as a communications expert at various global companies, and more than a decade after receiving my MBA from Johns Hopkins. My decision to simultaneously work and earn my doctorate felt like the biggest, boldest, most important move I could make for my career. I was pushing myself to my limits, juggling work, career, and family obligations.

At that time, everywhere I looked, I saw a troubling conversation brewing in the workplace. I wanted to participate in the dialogue. I knew I could do and contribute more.

I heard reports that most baby boomers will be retirement age eligible by 2030—by then, millennials and Generation Z will have officially taken over the workforce. If you've ever worked in an office environment of baby boomers and millennials, you may have noticed some *major* generational challenges related to communication, promotions, and organizational culture. A big part of my role at the time of these reports was helping executives communicate well with our employees, customers, and other stakeholders. Everything I read about generational differences had an unhelpful, negative outlook. I decided to focus my doctoral studies on how these generational issues might affect the workforce in a productive way. I wanted to understand how to make these interactions valuable, to share my solutions as a guide and help as many people as possible work through challenges effectively.

Sounds good, right? I thought so too. *But wait. There's more.*

I was fascinated by the role of women in the workplace. The data said we were "advancing" in our roles, but there was a major disparity between what we made and what our male counterparts made. Job retention was more challenging for women than for men due to caregiver and maternity leave obligations. In spite of this, almost all the women I knew were working hard to advance in their careers—and many of us were frustrated by what we considered unfair barriers to entry. As women began increasing our presence in management and roles previously dominated by men, I felt the shift in the baby boomer retirement population could be an opportunity to accelerate the advancement of women.

After years of dedicating myself to these areas and conducting studies and interviews, I ultimately reached out to a mentor who was an expert in the field of women's leadership development. I dialed into our conference call, a new doctor of management, feeling confident that she and I could be a dream team in helping women across generations advance in their careers. I was fully expecting her to say, "Yes! I can't wait to work together! We need more people like you doing this work!"

Let's just say I couldn't have been more wrong.

"Women lack self-efficacy," she told me with a sigh. "Women hold themselves back. Women don't really believe their efforts will pay off, so they don't try—it's well documented. Nothing can be done about this. Oh, and the generational context you've been studying? That means nothing. Sorry, Candace, but your work is a waste of time."

Wait, what?! Excuse me?!

I left that conversation embarrassed, angry, and confused. Did I mention I'd just paid for a doctoral degree? What had I gotten so wrong here?

I spent some time wondering how I'd so completely missed the mark, but after a few weeks of feeling disappointed in my mentor, I realized something about her sentiment just didn't feel right to me.

Her opinion was not my reality. I had to reject it.

We all know or have heard about successful women.

We all know a woman—maybe it's you—who has so much potential to advance in her career but hasn't. Or can't. Or won't.

We all know a woman—maybe it's you—who has deep regrets around risks she didn't take and chances she gave up.

We all know a woman—maybe it's you—who looks back on her life and wishes she'd been smarter with her time, her money, her opportunities, and her education.

We all know a woman—maybe it's you—who chose to put raising her family first. Now that she has delivered for them, it is time for her to pursue her dreams—but she doesn't know where to start and lacks support.

We all know a woman—maybe it's you—who has excelled in her career and now wants more or something different.

We all know a woman—maybe it's you—who isn't willing or ready to, or simply can't, give up on herself.

Surely there is a way through self-efficacy. Shouldn't we at least try?

Self-efficacy—a person's belief in themselves and their ability to achieve their desired outcome—is challenging for women. In truth, we are hardwired by cultural norms and expectations to exhibit self-defeating behaviors in life and our careers. For my mentor to dismiss these experiences by implying that women just "lacked" skills such as self-advocacy was too defeatist.

Not only that, but I couldn't shake my frustration at the idea that generational context is somehow irrelevant to career advancement. This simply cannot be right. Historically, when you were born shapes your values and ideas. Imagine how your life would be different if you'd grown up with a smartphone. Or without one. During a war. During a time of peace. With social media. Without it. Generational context affects how we see the world and interact with others, and there's no way that those differences don't affect our daily lives and how we conduct ourselves at work.

For me, the reality of the self-efficacy challenges women face shouldn't mean that we take no steps to create the future we want for ourselves. I propose that we take steps to protect and boost our self-efficacy. This means that sometimes we need a playbook, a framework, or a toolkit to help us navigate the unfortunate realities that come from being a woman in the workplace.

Think of it this way: In life, when we need help, we ask for it. It's the same thing when we are met with challenges at work.

To be honest, I'm actually thankful to this mentor for discouraging me that day on the phone. By questioning the validity of what I'd been studying, she helped me put my work into a more definitive focus. I had the confidence in myself and the data from my research to know she was off base. Women's lack of advancement cannot be solely credited to a simple (and patronizing) "lack of self-efficacy." It is much more complicated than that. I wasn't born with a silver spoon in my mouth, and as an African American female there have been many times where I felt the odds were not in my favor, yet I've been successful. I know a lot of women who've achieved great things in a myriad of careers and industries, and we haven't led charmed lives.

Many of us break through, and more of us need to achieve the careers we've earned and deserved. I know I can't fix all the obstacles women face while building their careers, but I do know that with the right tools in place, I can try to help women achieve levels of success—both professional and personal—that they never dreamed were possible.

I started by conducting a study to learn what matters to men and women at work. From my research findings, taken from about one thousand people, I established a list of the themes that connect all of us—male, female, old, and young—in our professional lives:

- Promotion: being recognized, valued, and advanced
- Performance: putting forth our best work
- Money: receiving financial compensation
- Balance: maintaining acceptable work/life balance
- Career: pivoting toward a new trajectory
- Retirement: ending our career journey[2]

Practically speaking, these themes connect every single working person, no matter their gender or age. The difference, found in my research, lies in prioritization.

Here's what I discovered. In general, women prioritize their performance above all else. Women want to feel like they are putting forth their very best work. This is true across multiple generations, from baby boomers to Gen Z.

Men, however? Gen X, millennial, and Gen Z men tend to prioritize making money. They want to get paid, and compensation plays a major role in their professional values. And baby boomer men tend to prioritize retirement above all else. They're focused on the long game, with the result being their personal stability and comfort.

These are intriguing findings, especially when you consider the pay gap that still exists between men and women. Every company wants their employees to perform well. Shouldn't this mean that, by and large, women are outperforming men, and therefore should be paid more based on performance alone?

Yes and no.

While women might be putting forth outstanding work, there are gaps aside from limitations from their boss, company, or family obligations. They may not be taking a long-term view of their careers.

2 Steele Flippin, C. (2017). *Generation Z in the workplace: helping the newest generation in the workforce build successful working relationships and career paths.*

They may lack clarity about what they need to achieve in their current roles, or are unclear about how roles might open doors for future skills and promotions. They may not understand how to access the privilege afforded most of their male counterparts to develop their skills on a continual basis.

In short, women are doing their jobs really, really well. They just don't always prioritize putting themselves in a position to translate those excellent job performances into the promotions, paychecks, and careers they deserve.

As I set forth conducting the research for this book, I spoke to thousands of women about their own career journeys. (I have included several of their quotes throughout the book.) I was surprised to hear from women who simply never got any career advice when they were starting out. Not from a mentor, not even from a friend. They felt totally alone, setting sail in their careers with no tools to steer their ship.

If you are a woman and nodding your head along with me right now, I think I know what you need and what may help you.

Do any of these scenarios ring true? Perhaps you need a stronger professional foundation. Maybe you need to know how to negotiate for the things that are important to you. Is it possible you need to be recognized for your excellent work? Do you need to know how to speak up for yourself, to have your opinions validated and heard? Maybe you need to know how to stick it out when times are tough at work. Or do you want some sort of toolkit to keep you accountable on your career path?

Simply put, you need to know exactly how to set yourself up for success—not just for the life of a certain project or role, but for the entire journey of the career path that you shape.

I am a doctor (of management), after all—you can consider this book my "career prescription" to help you do this for yourself.

The SHAPE acronym (i.e., Save, Hard Work, Advocate, Persevere, Educate) comes from years of research and my own personal experience working with young and midcareer professionals, strategizing with my peers, and speaking with my own mentors. You can take it all together or select small doses from each section.

S – Save
Create and nurture a strong financial future for yourself

H – Hard Work
Gain alignment with your boss on your impact

A – Advocate
Stand up for yourself, put yourself out there, speak up, and get noticed

P – Persevere
Keep going, keep trying, and know when it's time to leave

E – Educate
Continually advance your knowledge base and
improve upon your skillset(s)

You may not be alone. Lots of companies and organizations are making positive strides in these efforts. They want to keep great employees like you! But whether you are a woman just embarking on your career or a woman with years of experience behind you, you cannot rely on your employer to provide this training for you. If you are a female business owner yourself, you are probably nodding your head in agreement. You're busy trying to keep your business profitable and thriving!

It is in everyone's best interest if employees take control of their own career journeys—including you. Let's face it, resources are limited and not all managers invest in developing their people. Even if a company had all the best intentions, the best programs, and the best facilitators, it would take a long time for this message to reach everyone.

By picking up this book, you've started on your own journey toward financial, personal, and professional success. Just by taking this first step, you're already on the SHAPE path. You have decided that it is time for you to learn how to boost and manage your self-efficacy. You'll find each chapter packed with stories of women who are doing well, stories of women who have made mistakes, ideas for your current job situation no matter how far along you are in your career, and a toolkit to know when you are moving from the early stages of development into the expert behaviors.

Now is the time for *you* to take control of your present, and in turn, your future. It's time for *you* to set yourself up for success.

Ladies—it's time to get your career in SHAPE!

How to Apply the SHAPE Framework

In order for you to find success using the SHAPE framework, we need to get clear about one thing first:

A key ingredient to lasting success in your career is not just self-confidence, it's having strong self-efficacy.

But what *is* self-efficacy, anyway?

Generally speaking, self-efficacy is the belief a person holds in themselves and their ability to achieve the outcome they want. Simply put, if you believe that you will achieve your goal, you will attempt something, and if you don't think you will be successful—you won't even try. In a career context, having high or low self-efficacy can affect your performance.[3]

For example, have you ever not applied for a job or promotion because you didn't think you were ready—even though people around you like your boss or mentor assured you otherwise? Or even better, have you boldly moved forward to pursue a new endeavor despite naysayers? Did you refuse to doubt your ability to be successful in a task or job because your training and experience suggested otherwise? These are examples of how self-efficacy swoops in to limit or fortify your career trajectory.

---

3 Bandura, A. (1977). Self-efficacy: Toward a unifying theory of behavioral change. *Psychological Review*, 84(2), 191–215.

Having high self-efficacy takes self-confidence—your belief in your abilities—to the next level.

Implementing the SHAPE Framework

While deep-seated issues like institutional gender bias, sexism, and forms of self-policing continue to afflict professional women's self-efficacy, the SHAPE career framework—if truly put into practice—offers a model for women interested in strategies to improve not only their careers but also their work/life balance.

In addition, the reality of issues like burnout is beginning to feature more prominently in conversations concerning women's occupational self-efficacy.[4] Insights into career frameworks for women should address both tangible and intangible factors affecting women's career decisions from top to bottom.

The SHAPE career framework does just this by providing an accessible career approach designed to help you build up and practice enhancing your self-efficacy. As with any goal, gaining the confidence to put new knowledge and skills into practice is necessary for any program attempting to build women's occupational self-efficacy.

The Self-Efficacy Conundrum

It can be tempting to look at a successful, seemingly confident woman and assume she has mastered the art of keeping her self-efficacy intact or high. When I think about the mentor who shut me down all those years ago, I can see how, on the surface, she would have fit the exact picture of a woman who "made it." I learned later that, in that moment, she was projecting her own doubts and fears onto me. As I listened to her tell me that my work wasn't valuable, it would have been easy for me to say, "Well, I guess this is it. Time to throw in the towel, acknowledge my mistake in pursuing this work, and stop."

---

4 Occupational self-efficacy, defined as belief in one's ability to do one's job.
Schyns, B., & von Collani, G. (2002). A new occupational self-efficacy scale and its relation to personality constructs and organizational variables. *European Journal of Work and Organizational Psychology*, 11(2), 219–241

I couldn't do that. I believed in myself and my work, but there was more to it. Her discouraging remarks said much more about *her* than they did about *me*. She was entitled to her opinion; however, I am responsible for my choices and actions. I understood that, while I couldn't "fix" what led this woman to pass the brunt of whatever her past pain was onto me, I could recognize three critical aspects of success that I knew to be fundamental:

1. **Our ability to believe in and take a chance on ourselves is influenced by our mindset, and shaped by the examples we've seen in our formative years.** If you grew up seeing women take a back seat to men, that is bound to affect how you see yourself and believe in your skills and worth. If you've not seen someone recover from disappointment or experienced that yourself, it may diminish your ability to hope for better outcomes. If you've seen women rewarded for taking risks, speaking out, and being successful against odds, it frames your expectation for yourself. Likewise, if you grew up watching women use their voices to advocate for themselves consistently, that's going to show in how you stand up for yourself. In your next staff meeting, watch how women in their twenties assert themselves compared to women in their fifties, and you'll see what I mean.

2. **You don't have to go it alone. Be open to seeking and accepting help.** The effort required to keep your self-efficacy strong can be a bumpy ride full of stops and starts, riddled with self-realization, self-doubt, courage, and fear. We know from research that women with a strong mentor, whether that's a person or a group of people, are much more likely to be successful in their careers overall. It is essential to foster relationships to help you navigate all the ups and downs of your career if you struggle to help *yourself*. Note that you can and *should* also seek advice

from men. I often say, "If you want to win at football, you can't show up with a basketball playbook." You have to know how the game is played, so get advice from those who the game was made for to set yourself up to succeed.

3. **You have the power to choose how you manage your career. Believe it or not, your career isn't a final destination. It's a journey.** There are going to be times when it seems like you can't achieve what you want. There are going to be times when you feel unsure or even afraid that you are not ready for or worthy of your role. Some people call it imposter syndrome—although you are talented, you doubt yourself and feel like a fraud. In those inevitable moments, you have the power to choose how to move forward. You can choose to step forth and lead. You can choose to do nothing, which is *still a choice*. It's up to you. This book is about empowering you to make informed choices along your career journey.

I have mentored many women who hear this advice and nod their heads in agreement, then get stuck in old habits that hold them back. I'll admit, sometimes it's really easy to wallow in self-pity when your career journey takes you down an unanticipated, challenging road. Sometimes it is convenient to blame your boss, the culture, the myriad institutional barriers designed to hold women back, or any of the "isms" that shift the focus from what you yourself can control. Sometimes the brick wall is real, and you can't see yourself over, under, around, or through it. Even so, I encourage you to try.

I want you to be conscious of those knee-jerk reactions as you read this book and apply the SHAPE framework to your career.

Self-Efficacy Check Questionnaire

To understand where you are in your self-efficacy journey, ask yourself the questions below.[5] If you believe your responses may be holding your career back, this book is for you.

Am I stuck? For example, when faced with a tough assignment, you can't see your way through or ask for help. You spin wheels and stress out until the house of cards you've built comes crashing down on you.

Do I get my feelings hurt easily? For example, if someone disagrees with you, you shut down or withdraw without stating your case, even though everything inside tells you that you are right.

Do I get easily overwhelmed and freeze or give up? For example, you become easily distracted from achieving your goals or dreams because someone criticizes you or throws a past defeat in your face.

Do I become paralyzed when life throws me curveballs? For example, you can't or won't come up with a plan B or bounce back when unexpected life events get in the way of your plans. You stay in a bad or less than ideal job, relationship, or marriage because it is easier than dealing with the situation at hand.

Do I live in fear? For example, you are so scared of failure that you don't even try to apply for a promotion or a new job, even though you have a solid education and/or an excellent track record of success.

---

5 Adapted from Schwarzer, R., & Jerusalem, M. (1995). Generalized self-efficacy scale. In J. Weinman, S. Wright, and M. Johnston (Eds.), *Measures in health psychology: A user's portfolio. Causal and control beliefs* (35-37). Windsor, UK: NFER-Nelson.
Schwarzer, R., & Jerusalem, M. (2004). General self-efficacy scale. In S. Salek (Ed.), *Compendium of quality of life instruments*, 6(2A:1). Centre for Socioeconomic Research, Cardiff University; Euromed Communications. [CD- ROM publication, without page numbers].

Do I remain silent? For example, you do nothing about your exhausting frustrations—being marginalized, ignored, and dumped on—except complain to those who can't help you. Or you listen to their sound advice and choose not to follow it because complaining is easier.

Do I struggle to show any sign of leadership? For example, you can't cope during a crisis at work, get caught up in drama, and can't keep yourself steady in tough situations. No one looks to you for strength.

Do I find it difficult to be flexible? For example, you only have one go-to method of problem-solving, and when that fails, you can't find a solution. Worse, your pride won't let you ask for help or admit a mistake. You feel trapped.

Do I give off the impression of being inadequate? For example, you genuinely believe that you are fragile. You have a voice in your head telling you you're not good enough, so you can't save or help yourself when faced with opportunities or challenges.

Do I fear change? For example, you haven't quite reached your goal(s) within your timeframe, so you don't dare tempt fate by pursuing a new opportunity that may in fact be better than the artificial timeline you created for yourself.

In reality, we may all answer yes to these questions from time to time. Ask yourself, are you allowing these areas to hold you back from the career you want and deserve? Again, this work is about more than just self-confidence. You can have loads of confidence in your abilities but still lack the skills you need to translate those abilities into success. This is why I'm so focused on helping women become better at strengthening their self-efficacy. It's an essential key to unlocking all the doors we are bound to encounter in our careers.

It is often said that perception is reality. My research proves this to be as true for self-efficacy as it is for anything else. There is no way any of us can control our past or any number of our present circumstances. I certainly can't make it so you'll always look in the mirror and see perfection, nor would I want to.

That's not the point of my research.

What I want is for you to look objectively at where you've come from, focus clearly on where you're going, and have the confidence in your skills and ability to affect, influence, or create the change you need to get there. What I know through my own experience and the experience of so many others is this: finding a way to keep yourself accountable for this work is key to your SHAPE journey.

Getting to the Green Career Zone Behaviors

While I will be sharing many stories, findings from other studies related to women, and concepts from my research with you throughout this book, you'll notice that each chapter in the SHAPE framework will have a section called "Your Career Zone: Where are you now?" These sections have assessment charts that were designed to show you the mindset you might need to address before moving forward, depending on your circumstances.

This journey may not be a straight line for you. The intention is for you to recognize where you are based on any number of circumstances and look ahead to where you might be going. The colors will be a visual indicator that you are moving toward self-efficacy and the mindset to position yourself for the career you want and deserve.

Red, Yellow, and Green Career Zone Behaviors

I use the colors Red, Yellow, and Green as markers for the SHAPE framework in each chapter as defined below:

Red Career Zone	Yellow Career Zone	Green Career Zone
If you are in the Red career zone, you're just beginning. You are still coming to terms with what it means to be your own advocate in your career and just starting to map out a plan.	If you are in the Yellow career zone, you are taking strides toward the career you want and deserve.	If you are in the Green career zone, you are in the consistent habit of applying the SHAPE method to your career journey.
You may think: *I'm overwhelmed*, or *I can't do this.*	You may think: *I can do this*, or *I will do this.*	You may think: *I got this*, or *I am well on my way there.*
Your friends may say to you: *Come on?! You need to do this.*	Your friends may say to you: *You got this!*	Your friends may say to you: *You go!*

You may be tempted to jump directly past the process of self-reflection and into the "Green" career zone. Some of you may identify with aspects of each section in the framework. Again, I want to remind you that this is a journey, not a race. One of the most important things you will need to give yourself is grace. There is growth and career progression in trying new things, getting into new habits, making mistakes, and learning from them along the way.

This framework isn't a "to do" list. You will not be checking off boxes in each zone. That's not how this journey works. You are writing your own career plan. Be kind to yourself. You are the best judge of how you want or need to boost your self-efficacy. In some cases, you might only need to do one or two things differently to move into the "Green" category. For others, you might be stuck in the "Red" or "Yellow" for a while as you work through undoing some intense underlying challenges. Choose for yourself. And remember to keep going.

At the end of each chapter, I offer the key takeaways as a reference. I recommend that you share your journey with others. To help you, I also provide some questions in case you want to form a support circle or reading group to share your career development and growth experience with others for encouragement and guidance.

I cannot promise perfection in your career journey. I hope that by using the tools and frameworks included in this book, you'll find that your career, and ultimately your success, will be possible in ways you might not have imagined.

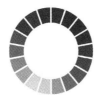

CHAPTER 1:
SAVE YOUR MONEY SO FINANCES WON'T GET IN THE WAY OF YOUR CAREER OPTIONS

"I am overwhelmed by student loan bills, paying off my car, and insurance."

—Maria, millennial, sales representative

I start my SHAPE framework with *Saving*. Having enough money is an essential aspect in many areas of life. Through my research and in my own life, I also learned that the level to which you have a solid financial foundation impacts your self-efficacy.

When I was twenty-five years old, I believed I had it all figured out. I had a great job, enough money to afford the lifestyle I wanted, and a fiancé I couldn't wait to marry.

All right, fine. That's not totally true. I had a good job, but I was just starting out. I could envision myself getting promotions, yet those would be a long way (and a lot of work) down the road. And money? Well, I was making it, but spending more than I was making. That's what my eleven credit cards were for.

You read that correctly. Eleven credit cards.

I wasn't unlike so many young women at the start of their careers—spending more than I made, but preparing for a lifestyle that would solve any of the unfortunate financial messes I found myself in. After all, I was paying my bills on time. I made my minimum credit card payments. And I was marrying my best friend! Once our finances were combined, all my problems would be solved.

At twenty-five years young, I felt so blessed to be marrying my best friend, convinced that everything in my life was on track. Unlike many of our friends, who wanted to remain in our beloved hometown of Detroit after college, my fiancé Dwayne and I were planning to move to Washington, DC, to live in the capital. We wanted to change the world. He had already secured a role starting in January, and I planned to follow him in March of that year to launch our power couple journey.

I had already given my leave notice to my boss and landlord. I was scouring job postings and reaching out to people in my network to talk about opportunities. My prospects looked good. My wedding plans were underway—I started looking at potential wedding venues, thinking about the caterers. I increased my workout frequency so my curves could fit into my dream wedding dress. We'd go back and forth in our conversations about our new life. I wanted more, he wanted less. I wanted to be in the center of the city's action, and he wanted to live just outside city limits so he didn't have too long of a commute. It felt like happy stress as we worked through the details.

Life, however, had other plans.

Just a few days before Christmas, at 4:00 a.m. on December 19, I received a call from my sorority sister. She told me, choking through tears, that Dwayne had died in a car accident and that I needed to get to the hospital right away to meet his family.

As I sat in the waiting room holding back my tears, grief, and devastation, I tried to comfort Dwayne's family. I felt numb. One of my biggest champions, my best friend, was gone. My carefully laid future had evaporated before my eyes, all my life plans that had intertwined with his goals gone. And I had to swallow yet another devastating pill: our living arrangements and expenses had been planned around a two-income household, which he would be footing the bill for until I secured a job. He was a significant part of my plan and support system.

When he died, so did our plans.

Dwayne often told me that he loved me because I was strong and independent, and that nothing could stop me. Yet I felt like a fraud—like I was letting both of us down all those sleepless teary nights as I struggled to work through the pain and get back toward my potential. So many women told me my life was over, to prepare myself for an existence of misery following my devastating loss. I often told myself that yes, he had died, but not my dreams and aspirations—I committed to keep moving forward. It took me two years to get to Washington, DC. I had to work through my grief, save money, develop a new career plan, and start over—alone. Though I made it, it was a long, hard road.

I tell women this story for a couple reasons. First and foremost, it's a reminder that each and every day is precious. Cultivate your relationships and never take them for granted. I'm happily married today with an awesome family, and I often remind women that things do work out.

This is not just a message for young women. "Life" happens to all of us, and these ups and downs we face constantly impact our career trajectory. There is much we cannot control, but we can control the steps we take to build our financial foundations. We can start by choosing to do something. And at any time in your career, your savings or lack thereof will play a role in your journey.

The Savings Continuum

You don't have to take my word for it. A considerable amount of scholarly literature, practitioner studies, and news media coverage says that lack of financial literacy is a major hindrance to advancement in the workplace—and overall life satisfaction.

A 2019 study asked why, with issues surrounding female empowerment so prevalent in society, women struggle to attain confidence and make informed monetary decisions.[6] Here's what they found:

- Today's women are experiencing unique challenges to attaining financial confidence, including

  * fewer women with earning power (in 2013, 60 percent of women had earning power; in 2019, this number had dropped to 38 percent)

  * fewer women who report having more earning power (between 2013 and 2019, women's earning power dropped from 57 percent to 46 percent)

  * fewer women who say they are the chief financial officer of their household (53 percent in 2013 compared to 47 percent in 2019)

- Fewer women say they have asked for a promotion or a raise at work (27 percent in 2019 compared to 44 percent in 2016). Many also say they feel less financially secure overall (62 percent in 2019 versus 68 percent in 2016).

It's not that we don't want to be more financially literate: 57 percent of the women in the study expressed a desire to be more confident in their financial choices.

---

6 Allianz Life. (2019). Despite rising influence, women report steady decline in financial confidence. *BusinessWire*. https://www.businesswire.com/news/home/20190624005422/en/ Despite- Rising-Influence-Women-Report-Steady-Decline-in-Financial-Confidence

As with so many things in our lives, it's complicated. Generational differences and marital status play a key role in women's self-confidence as it relates to money, with millennial and divorced women reporting higher rates of monetary stability and self-efficacy. Although working with financial professionals also features prominently in the study, many women report feelings of disempowerment when their financial planners do not treat them as the decision-maker. In other words, societal gender expectations continue to dictate that women are not the financial decision-makers in their household—and this erodes women's confidence in making big life decisions.

Many financial institutions such as Bank of America, Chase, Fifth Third, First Horizon, Truist, and Wells Fargo recognize this problem and have sponsored financial literacy programs aimed to help women. Recent news reports show that the COVID-19 pandemic has also set women back. Yet, regardless of obstacles within the financial education system, women who are not educated about economics and finance feel the effects of it in many ways:

- They feel a lack of confidence in themselves, which translates into a lack of confidence in their work performances.

- They feel less empowered to make important career choices such as changing jobs or starting their own businesses.

- They shy away from making important life decisions for themselves because they are unfamiliar with financial terms.

In other words, a lack of financial literacy can directly hold a woman back from reaching her full potential.

This is certainly the place I found myself in when my fiancé died. After I had allowed myself time to process my grief and my new "reality," I focused on my career. I reminded myself often that the best way I could honor Dwayne's memory and move on with my life was to pick myself up and move forward as the strong, brave woman he knew me to be.

I did just that. I had a great job and a rental I loved. But by the time I was thirty, I was ready for more. I wanted to buy a home.

Buying a home involves a lot more than just a 20 percent down payment, which I didn't have. I realized as I started the process that I was lacking some basic financial literacy that would make a huge impact on my future:

- I didn't know that my credit score wasn't high enough to get the best rates, and that a good credit score is crucial to securing a good long-term loan.

- I didn't realize that by having a relationship with an actual banker at my bank, I might be given access to some first-time home buyer assistance programs, through my lender or via government-sponsored programs.

- I didn't fully appreciate how defeated I would feel knowing that my poor financial decisions would mean that I could not choose to live where I wanted.

- I didn't understand that the price for those actions was lost time in my day and the added sacrifice of a significant commute to my already grueling work schedule.

You'll notice these are not things that I figured out in an afternoon. It was a long process of saving, getting smart about what I could afford and what I wanted to afford, and considering all the little things I could do along the way to make myself a good candidate for a long-term loan.

If you are just starting out on this savings continuum and feeling overwhelmed, I have good news for you. Just like your career, your financial literacy is also a journey. Here are some of the small ways I see women take control of their financial literacy in ways that dramatically impact their success and future:

- **They don't spend more than they take home every month.** Yes, I know, this one seems obvious. It's also hard, especially when you're young and the women around you are making different decisions with their money. But trust me, getting into this habit is the key to financial independence and success.

- **They read the fine print.** It is easy to fall victim to a "great deal," especially if it's something you really want. But when it comes to credit cards, a line of credit, a payment plan, or any other offer that seems too good to be true, it's imperative that we stop and make sure we understand who really benefits from this deal in the long run.

- **They save.** We will talk much more about this in the next section, but getting into the habit of saving every single month is both easy and beneficial for the life of your career.

- **They have an emergency plan.** We never know when something unexpected will happen. Whether it's a surprise household expense, the end of a relationship, the loss of a job, a global pandemic, or a great business opportunity that requires an investment, having an emergency fund to tap into will reduce the strain of paying an unexpected bill. Most American women are forced to acquire debt to get through the tough times, which can become a vicious cycle: credit card interest accrues over time, making it more difficult to get out of debt. Having emergency money set aside eliminates—or at least reduces—the need to acquire debt during a tough time in your life. You can also avoid a dual dilemma of first dealing with the emergency, then grappling with the aftermath of increased debt.

More Than Money

Getting into good financial habits is a long, continuous journey that is about more than money. It's about setting up the foundation you'll need when you do find yourself at a crossroads—whether by circumstance, luck, or some other unforeseen fork in the road—so you'll be able to make decisions based on what you want, as opposed to what your wallet dictates.

For example, after working hard and buying a home, I looked like the picture of success. To a degree, that was true. I was (and still am!) so proud of all I'd accomplished even with having to navigate the tragic loss of Dwayne. And then, I was offered my dream job: the role of executive director of an organization dedicated to increasing the number of young voters. I would be on the ground, shaping and driving the change I personally wanted to see for a cause that I genuinely believed in. I was so excited to engage in this meaningful work.

Unfortunately, the salary was 10 percent less than what I was making at the time. Taking the pay cut would have devastated me financially. I had to turn it down.

I lamented that opportunity for months after. One afternoon, I confided in my friend Rick that I wished I could have taken the job. "I just couldn't make the numbers work," I told him sadly. "I mean, if I had savings, then maybe . . ."

Rick's expression changed.

"Candace," he said. "Yes, you're young, successful, and single. But anything can happen to you—your life can change in an instant. Why on earth don't you have at least three months of your living expenses in your savings account *at all times?*"

I was embarrassed. In my mind, I was making financial sacrifices all the time. I was paying my mortgage and my bills, and I was skipping out on vacations I couldn't afford. Sure, my credit card debt was high, but I was making those payments, slowly.

I hated feeling that my career goals were unattainable because of my uninformed choices. I realized that I saved episodically for important expenses, like the down payment on my house. But I hadn't made saving for my life and future in general a priority. The truth I didn't want to admit was that there was a lot I could still do. There was a lot I was still putting off. There were plenty of ways I could take control of my life financially and set myself up so that the next time my dream job came up, I wouldn't have to worry about a pay decrease and could say yes on the spot.

Special Challenges Facing Women

Anyone can and will face challenges on the road to financial literacy, but women can face unique obstacles they must overcome to feel truly "free" financially.

1. **We still aren't compensated fairly.** According to the US Department of Labor, women in the workforce are gaining in numbers compared to men. We are earning more degrees. Yet we still make eighty-one cents on the dollar compared to men's wages, and we lag behind men in representation in top leadership roles. This deficit can be difficult to overcome and places many women behind men in their lifetime earnings—and subsequently, their savings ability.

2. **We may be overwhelmed with debt.** High credit card balances are considered indicators of financial illiteracy, with women engaging in significantly more costly spending behaviors than men.[7] In contrast, both men and women who rank as financially literate tend to have lower rates of credit card debt.[8]

3. **We may be waiting for our knight in shining armor to save us.** Having a partner who takes care of the finances and household expenses is terrific. Being a stay-at-home mom or housewife fills noble and important roles. Period. However, this lifestyle choice does not happen for most women. My re-

7 Mottola, G. (2012). *In our best interest: Women, financial literacy, and credit card behavior.* FINRA Investor Education Foundation: Insights Financial Capabilities. http://dx.doi.org/10.5038/1936-4660.6.2.4

8 Mottola, G. (2012). *In our best interest: Women, financial literacy, and credit card behavior.* FINRA Investor Education Foundation: Insights Financial Capabilities. http://dx.doi.org/10.5038/1936-4660.6.2.4

cent research shows that more than half of women today are the primary breadwinners in their households. According to the Pew Research Center, about two-thirds of married people who lived with their spouse before getting married saw it as a step toward marriage. However, another study found that approximately 20 percent of engagements don't result in marriage,[9] and the current divorce rate is about 40 percent.[10] These statistics are stark realities to be prepared for if the housewife approach can't or doesn't work out.

4. **We've lost an income source we've relied on.** "Four times as many women as men dropped out of the labor force in 2020 after September, roughly 865,000 women compared with 216,000 men," due to the COVID-19 pandemic.[11] When someone has recently lost a job or has been unemployed for an extended period, it can be a blow. A recent divorce or separation can also exhaust emergency savings. If a partner who contributes to household expenses has lost his or her job, that household may have limited or no other available resources. Health issues, such as a physical disability or a mental or chronic illness, may also limit a person's ability to work and earn an income. A chronic condition or other illness that requires many resources and income to maintain, sustain, or prolong health can drain discretionary income. Health issues may involve being called upon to be a caregiver for a sick parent, spouse, retirement partner, or child. Regardless of the cause, losing the primary sources of income limits the ability to save and can be challenging to navigate.

9 Bruk, D. (2018). *20 Percent of all weddings are called off—here's why.* BestLife. https://bestlifeonline.com/engagements-called-off-break-up-stories/

10 Luscombe, B. (2018). The divorce rate is dropping. That may not actually be good news. *Time.* https://time.com/5434949/divorce-rate-children-marriage-benefits/

11 Kashen, J., Glynn, S. J., & Novello, A. (2020). *How COVID-19 sent women's workforce progress backward.* Center for American Progress. https://www. americanprogress.org/issues/women/reports/2020/10/30/492582/covid-19-sent-womens- workforce-progress-backward/

5. **We participate in negative self-talk.** Maybe you're one of those people who, for your whole life, has been told that you can't save, that you're a poor saver, or that you're a financial black sheep. Over time, you come to accept these statements about yourself as true. If you take nothing else from this chapter, take this: you are not doing yourself any favors by speaking about yourself in this way. You can do this work if you choose to. It's that simple.

Practical Savings

Don't worry, this book isn't going to tell you that you should never enjoy yourself or treat yourself to something you deserve. In fact, I believe that depriving yourself of all joy in your life just so you can have a bigger bank account is a terrible way to live.

In my TEDx Talk "Are You Talking to Me? What Women Really Want . . . at Work," I advise women to save their money so they can have a solid financial foundation.

- **Have an emergency fund.** I suggest at least six months (preferably more) in living expenses so you can make decisions about your life and career that are not based on monetary fear. Make sure those funds are in an FDIC-insured bank account.

- **Know and understand your credit score.** In general, the better your credit score, the better rates you'll have, which could save you money over time. At some point, you may choose to apply for credit. Perhaps you need a loan for your primary residence. Maybe you need a credit card or a car, or there are other personal or household needs that you need to finance over a period of time. Understanding your credit score helps you understand your expectations for the rates that will be available to you. Your credit score can also impact your career, as employers check credit scores as a sign of your reliability, honesty, and ability to manage money.

- **Reinvest your raises into yourself.** Yes, you should celebrate your successes with a delicious meal and maybe a new necklace you've had your eye on. But after that, make sure you're not just spending all the money that comes your way in the form of a raise or bonus. For example, if you receive a 3 percent raise, put half of it toward your contribution to your retirement plan or your emergency savings. This approach allows you to save without changing your current spending habits.

- **Create a plan for your business.** If you are a small business owner, you must create a solid business plan. This allows entrepreneurs and business owners to understand their customers, market trends, competition, timing, and a whole host of other topics that contribute to success. If you're just getting started, or you launched your business based on your passion and didn't take time to put together a formal business plan, I recommend that you begin now. Set up a profit and loss sheet—be aware of your business's expenses and income. In your first years of business, you might need to operate on a shoestring budget before growing and expanding. You may also need to rely on your savings to pay your personal bills or business expenses during your startup period, so make sure you have at least six months' to one year's worth of savings before starting out.

- **Meet with a banker, tax, and financial advisor to understand your personal and business options and goals.** You may pay people to color your hair, take care of mowing your lawn, service your vehicle, walk or board your pet, provide you with health care services, or serve you a meal in lieu of cooking yourself. These are services that help make your life easier. The same logic applies to your finances. Invest and make the time to speak with professionals to give yourself the best chance for the most favorable financial foundation you can. While there are beneficial online financial resources available to consumers and business owners, they don't take the place of an actual human advisor. Meet with your advisor(s) regularly and as needed. This will ensure you are on track with your goals, have a balanced portfolio, and have an adequate understanding of your tax liabilities and how shifting market trends and interest can either impact or create a favorable opportunity for you.

- **Plan and save for retirement**. For some of you, retirement seems a million years away. Although the pandemic lowered life expectancy, you may end up living longer than you planned, which means we're going to spend upwards of two to three decades in retirement. One of the best ways to save for retirement is contributing to an employer plan, especially if your employer matches your contributions. If your employer does not provide retirement plans, or perhaps you're self-employed, consider a traditional IRA, Roth IRA, or Investment Development Account (IDA), a particular bank account that allows you to save for big-ticket items such as education, a home purchase, or starting a business.

- **Review your finances regularly**. Don't set and forget your budget and expenses! Remember, financial literacy is a journey that will depend on many different factors. That's why it's critical to stay on top of your spending habits and not make impulsive decisions with your money no matter where you are in your life or career phase.

Getting into the Green Career Zone Behaviors

It took me years and plenty of missteps to get to the place where I am today. There will always be barriers in front of you. Taking the right steps and getting into the right habits is a commitment to yourself and your overall success that you simply cannot skip.

Before we look at the chart to get into the Green Zone, be sure to do the following:

- **Set a timed goal.** For example, if you are $5,000 in credit card debt, commit to paying off at least half of that balance by the end of the year. If you're just starting out, commit to saving 10 to 20 percent of each of your paychecks in your emergency fund, starting the next pay cycle. Hold yourself accountable by telling people you know and trust about this goal.

- **Discuss.** Speaking of telling people you know and trust about your goals, you will also want to begin by having an honest conversation with whomever you share finances with. Be open about where you would like to see changes in your spending habits and how you hope to get there.

- **Seek advice.** There is so much to learn about financial literacy, and you do not want to go it alone. Seek help where you need it.

- **Read.** In order to get familiar with financial terms, you'll want to get in the habit of reading consumer-friendly publications or listening to podcasts about financial literacy. You can also take a financial literacy quiz to see where you can improve.

- **Understand your financial situation.** No matter whether you are just starting out or have shared finances with a partner for most of your adult life, now is the time to understand where your money is, how you spend it, and what you need to do to make your future more financially secure.

- **Know your worth.** Are you compensated appropriately for your contributions? Have you researched the current compensation or going rates for your products or services? Can you obtain objective feedback on your performance and the quality and competitiveness of your offering? Do you have mentors, advisors, or sponsors who can help you negotiate equitable terms? Can you improve your performance or acquire new skills to fill in gaps? Are you prepared to have the discussion with key decision-makers to make it right, as well as make the best decision for your life and career if you can't?

- **Review your finances regularly.** It's all too easy to let impulsive decisions erode your savings aside from your best intentions. Monitor your finances closely!

- **Business owner? Have three to six months of operating expenses.** The general rule of thumb is to have three to six months' worth of operating expenses in cash at any given time. Work with your financial advisor to understand the timeframe for your needs.

We will be talking much more about knowing your worth throughout this book. In the next chapter, we are going to focus on hard work. In the meantime, consider where you are in the status of your finances, and how you can move forward from what's holding you back.

Your Savings Career Zone: Where are you now?

Having a strong financial foundation is the backbone of your life and career. Do you have enough money to make independent and crucial decisions about your life and your career? Is your approach to managing your finances limiting your career? The colors Red, Yellow, and Green are visual indicators that you are moving in the right path toward strengthening your self-efficacy and building a mindset to position yourself for the career you want and deserve.

As you read the next chart, consider where you are in the framework and how you can start planning to move forward from what's holding you back and celebrate your progress.

Career Zone Assessment: Saving

Red Career Zone	Yellow Career Zone	Green Career Zone
• I am overwhelmed by debt. • Fear is holding me back. • I am afraid to ask for help. • I can't cope with my current lack of savings. • I have little to no emergency savings. • I live over my budget and constantly float on credit cards. • I don't invest in my retirement. • I am unaware of my credit score and how it might be affecting me. • I have little impulse control when it comes to spending. • I often say things like, "I'll figure out the money later."	• I have a support network I can ask for help. • I can reframe negative self-talk. • I believe I can change my current circumstance. • I am open to change. • My lack of savings doesn't define me. • I have three to six months' emergency savings. • I very rarely go over my monthly budget. • I contribute to a retirement plan. • I know I have a good credit score. • I have a vague understanding of household finances, but remain in the dark about some elements, like investing. • I feel confident that, if something major doesn't happen, I'll be okay.	• I am where I want to be with my savings and debt levels. • I proactively help bring others along. • I can embrace change. • I believe this situation too shall pass. • I have a plan B. • I have one year or more of emergency savings. • I never go over budget. • I practice very healthy spending habits. • I meet with a financial planner regularly. • I have a balanced portfolio. • I have an estate plan. • I have an excellent credit score. • I have multiple streams of income. • I find it easy to delay gratification for purchases.

KEY CHAPTER TAKEAWAYS:

- Self-efficacy is increased when you take control of your financial foundation and make informed decisions about money.

- Your financial freedom is dependent upon your financial literacy.

- Financial literacy is a journey—take small steps and form healthy habits.

- There are special circumstances that make women more vulnerable to financial missteps than men. Be aware of those pitfalls and make your financial education a priority.

- If you are a business owner, you probably stepped out on faith to make your business dream a reality. Make it a priority to get your finances in order, including your compensation.

Questions for Further Discussion with Your Support Circle

While your finances are personal, having help along your journey can better prepare you to achieve your goals and help strengthen your outlook on your ability to achieve success. Consider forming a support circle or reading group. Working with a group of women you trust and respect can really help you put some of these financial best practices to work for you. Perhaps you can invite a banker or financial planning expert. Have a conversation, be open to new ideas and suggestions, and don't forget to download the accompanying workbook to help keep you accountable.

What She Said . . . Reflections from Women

Sometimes it can be difficult to begin a discussion about financial challenges. Below is a series of responses from the women in my study related to barriers to creating better financial health and greater wealth.

Do any of these statements ring true for you? Why or why not?

- *Jobs are very scarce in the area where I live. I need to be closer to the city for better opportunities.*

- *My husband spends more money than we make.*

- *I am a single mom and just can't seem to get ahead. I live paycheck to paycheck and wonder if I will never be financially safe.*

- *The only barrier is that I was unable to save more during the pandemic.*

- *I don't have experience in work fields—I'm young, and no one wants to hire without experience even if you have the qualities the job wants.*

- *It isn't helpful telling women about the gender wage gap within institutions but not advocating for or providing any route toward organization and mobilization to see change.*

- *I am overwhelmed by student loan bills, paying off my car, and insurance.*

Additional Questions to Consider:

- Are you satisfied with how you are managing your finances and savings? Why or why not?

- What are the reasons women consistently score lower on financial literacy tests compared to men?

- How can monetary education programs be designed to better serve the needs of women?

- How can men and women develop an equal understanding of finances?

- How can we prompt women to seek financial advice?

- How do we explain why men and women act differently with money?

- What role does age play in financial literacy?

- Would working women benefit from female-only financial education programs?

- How important is language in assessing women's financial literacy (e.g., using "masculine" terms or questionnaires like those that incorporate numerals)? If so, what are the barriers and opportunities for making women more confident with money?

- What role does market volatility play in women's financial literacy and overall financial self-efficacy?

- To what extent can gender differences be improved to increase overall levels of literacy in finance?

- How intentional are you in frequenting women-owned businesses?

- If you are a business owner, what are you doing to keep financial literacy a priority among your staff?

- How often are you networking with other business owners about financial opportunities for yourself?

- What resources or help do you need to launch, stabilize, or grow for business?

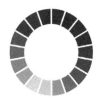

CHAPTER 2:
HARD WORK IS SUBJECTIVE—MAKE SURE YOU AND YOUR BOSS ARE ALIGNED

"Hard work does not necessarily equal success. You must be on the same page with whomever evaluates you about what exactly you must do to achieve your goals."

—Judith, baby boomer, information technology leader

———

You may have noticed that all the words in the SHAPE framework are represented by one word except for H, which stands for *Hard Work*. It was an intentional decision because that phrase kept showing up in my research. Whether they were asked what they regretted in their career or what advice they would give, many women wished that they could have cracked the code on hard work. It set me off on a journey to understand what was behind hard work and its role in self-efficacy—turns out that the level of alignment with your boss plays a key role.

I once mentored a talented woman I'll call Michelle. She was smart, capable, and eager to make her mark in her career. She shared stories of her parents, her home life, the sacrifices she'd made to get to the place she had, and her genuine gratitude for not having grown up with a silver spoon in her mouth.

She knew from her humble beginnings, as well as the rags-to-riches stories in the media and movies that defined her Generation X adolescence, that the key to success was pretty simple: work your tail off.

That's exactly what she did. It took her a couple years after college to land a job at her dream company, an architecture firm in Chicago, but when she finally did, she was elated. Every time we would connect via phone to catch up, she was running from one meeting to another, always juggling fifteen things at once. In her mind, she was checking off every box. She was doing all the right things. She was setting herself up for success.

In some ways, she was. I would never tell you that working hard isn't a good idea—it is! In fact, in my research, women regardless of generation group often say they wish they had worked harder when asked to reflect on their career.

In Michelle's case, however, after years of work, she learned that in her quest to do all the things that were asked of her, she'd never taken the time to articulate her goals to her boss. If she had, she would have learned that all the tasks she was completing were not putting her on the path toward the role she ultimately wanted at the company. She, like so many women, just assumed her boss knew she wanted to be promoted. She thought her hard work would speak for itself.

When her dream role at the company opened up, Michelle was sure it would go to her. Taking into account her years of sixty- to eighty-hour workweeks as well as the fact that she'd put her personal life and marital plans on hold, there was no way her hard work wouldn't be rewarded.

But the role went to someone else—a man with fewer skills and less experience. Crushed, Michelle met with her boss of nearly five years and demanded to know why she hadn't gotten the role.

"Michelle," he said, stunned, "every time we've talked about your career goals and aspirations, you've just expressed a desire for more work, which I've given you. When I asked you about promotions, you told me you weren't ready and needed a few more years to really understand your role. I had no idea you were interested in this promotion. I wish you would have told me!"

She and I spent hours reflecting on the conversation and her frustration with not getting the job. All she could point to was how unfair it all was.

Over time, she came to realize that her hard work *had* been noticed. She had great performance reviews and would often receive compliments from her peers. However, when her boss asked about her career plans during development meetings, she always said, "I just want to learn all I can, do a good job, and grow." She didn't say what was actually on her mind: *"One day, I want your job."* When he did mention a new role for her, she told him she needed more time to focus on her current position. When he tried to assign her leadership roles in projects, she insisted she was happy being a team player. When she received compliments for her achievements, she never said thank you and simply received the recognition, always downplaying the accolade and quickly giving credit to someone else: "It was a team effort," or "I guess I was just lucky that day."

Finally, her boss just stopped asking.

If Michelle's story rings a bell for you, you're not alone. This chapter will help you understand the fine line between working hard and working smart.

Balancing Work and Life: The Struggle Is Real

*"I think the cliche 'work hard and you will
succeed' is damaging because there are more
factors involved in success than just working hard.
It also implies that if you 'fail' it is because you
didn't work hard enough, which is a damaging
narrative."*

—Liz, Gen Z, analyst

Oftentimes, when I'm speaking to groups of women about career development and get to the H in the SHAPE method—hard work—they assume that I mean "work more." The discussion inevitably shifts to those women sharing the realities of everything on their plates that must be managed in or outside of work. My research isn't suggesting that women put in more or fewer hours—that's an important distinction as we move forward.

So many women are faced at some point or another with what feels like a major dilemma: choosing their family or choosing their career. Making each work is tough—both at once is even tougher. This challenge can manifest itself in many ways:

- juggling work responsibilities while caring for a sick or aging parent;
- prioritizing a spouse's career path over your own;
- keeping your career on track while dealing with a child who has special needs, a high-risk pregnancy, or taking extended time off after having a baby;
- dealing with the new normal from the pandemic;
- or any other of the multiple ways in which "life" throws a wrench into our best-laid career plans.

Throughout my career, I've spoken with so many women who face this dilemma. They are conflicted or feel guilty over leaving a career to begin raising or taking care of their family. Some have been uncertain, chosen the job, and later deeply regretted it. Don't get me wrong—if you *want* to choose your career over everything else, by all means do so. But first, take time and give yourself space to consider the trade-offs and impact of your decision. Have conversations with those in your life who are affected so that they are on the same page and can support you. As with all things, the decision might carry some consequences that you will need to rectify, address, and own. And please, don't "mom shame" those who choose to be a full-time mother, take a hybrid role, or have a full-time professional role.

If you own a business, this is especially important to remember as you help your employees navigate their career paths. Imagine how much harder it will be to achieve your business goals if you have a team of women who are miserable in their home lives!

Again, the choice is always yours. Just do what you can to make those choices with your eyes wide open.

"I have to share this section from Harvard Business Review *[2004] that I learned too late: There is a secret out there, a painful, well-kept secret: at midlife, between one-third and half of all successful career women in the United States do not have children. In fact, 33 percent of such women (business executives, doctors, lawyers, academics, and the like) in the forty-one-to-fifty-five age bracket are childless, and that figure rises to 42 percent in corporate America. These women have not chosen to remain childless. The vast majority yearn for children. Indeed, some have gone to extraordinary lengths to bring a baby into their lives. They subject themselves to complex*

medical procedures, shell out tens of thousands of dollars, and derail their careers."

—Sharon, Gen X, customer service director

"They tell women to put family first. This is more harmful because women hold back their careers to care for husbands, family, kids, etc., but never advocate for themselves."

—Keisha, millennial, sales vice president

This dilemma of "having it all" is unique to women. From a young age, we are told over and over again that the most successful women have the husband, the kids, the job, the salary, and somehow manage to make time for family dinner five nights a week. This is both an unrealistic and an unhealthy mindset for women to have, no matter where they are in their careers. Women manage their work and home lives in all kinds of different ways.

Some women choose to work forty hours or more a week and hire an amazing nanny for their children.

Some women are happy to choose their career.

Some women wake up one day and decide they want a different or new career.

Some women decide that taking time away from work altogether is the best choice for them.

Some women can make a part-time gig work when they must balance family obligations.

Some women step away from corporate life and choose entrepreneurship so they can have more control over their personal life and schedule.

Some women wouldn't choose a career over being at home for the world.

Some women have help and others don't.

Some women don't want to be married.

Some women don't want to raise children.

Some women can't have what they want.

Some women are just doing it all the best they can to make life work.

The point is simple: the choice you make needs to be the right choice for *you*. Lead with your peace of mind, your family's happiness, and your well-being.

I worked with a woman whose dream was to have a child. After several devastating miscarriages, she finally sat down with her employer and told them she needed to take time off to rest her body, rest her mind, and focus on creating the family she so desired.

This is what I mean when I talk about the importance of creating a mindset that is less driven to act (or not act) by fear. Was it difficult for this woman to have that conversation with her boss? Absolutely! But unlike Michelle, she knew the value of articulating her goals, and that ultimately, she was in charge of making her dream come true. Otherwise, she'd live to regret it. It was the best decision for her, and she now enjoys her children even more.

Fortunately, a tide is turning. An unforeseen gift of the COVID-19 pandemic is that many businesses have been forced to implement remote working schemes. Many more are assessing the demands they put on their employees when they ask them to juggle in-office schedules and stable home lives. Additionally, many women who have felt like they've "missed" so much of their family time due to job demands are seeing the benefits of being home more.

Make decisions for yourself, your family, and your career without apology. I'll be the first to tell you that everyone is going to have an opinion about the choices you make—try not to let those opinions weigh you down mentally. Don't worry about taking time away from work, and don't take a job you consider beneath your skillset or ability when you do make your way back to the workforce. Keep your network informed and try to create your own safety net.

We'll talk much more about "leaning in" later in this chapter, but until then, remember that you give yourself power when you live and lead with authenticity. Lean in if that's what you want. Step away if that's the right choice. Lead with being true to yourself, and it will be the right path for you.

The Kaleidoscope Career Model

Most people associate work with labor, either physical or mental. You put forth effort and get paid for that effort.

Simple, right? Not so fast.

For women, studies show that work is more personal. Women value roles that "work" for their lives, not just their careers. They are conscious of the toll their work might take on their home lives and families. Oftentimes, women are more careful to take on work that will allow for balance and avoid burnout. In addition, women take jobs based on what is compatible with their current or near-term life situations, rather than focusing solely on ambition or financial compensation.

In other words, they want roles that allow them the most freedom to choose the work-life balance that works for them.

This is known as the Kaleidoscope Career Model approach. Women value taking on roles that they can blend into their lives as they currently are and use to create a cohesive pattern of authenticity, balance, and challenge. Here's what that might look like:

- Maybe she takes on a part-time role instead of a full-time one.

- Maybe she starts her own company instead of trying to fit in somewhere else.

- Maybe she takes a sabbatical or extended leave for personal reasons, something her male counterparts may be less likely to do—while a third of Americans can't afford to take unpaid time off, men are offered more paid sabbaticals than women.[12]

---

12 eDreams. (2017). *American employees are rated the most burnt-out and overworked.* https://www.edreamsodigeo.com/wp-content/uploads/sites/19/2017/09/Sabbaticals-U.S.-14SEP17.pdf

- Maybe she leaves her job to raise her family or goes back to school to learn a skill that will better suit her home life.

Do men do this too? Certainly. But here's where it gets interesting. As the strains of working in their careers begin to catch up to them, women in their mid- to late careers gravitate toward authenticity in their work lives. Research suggests that women tend to pivot and focus on creating work arrangements that speak to their individuality. Here's what that might look like:

- Maybe she foregoes a promotion until her children are in elementary school and she can have more time in the day to focus.

- Maybe she switches from full time to part time to care for an aging parent.

- Maybe she'll take a lesser-paying job to shorten her commute so she can be home to cook dinner for her family sooner.

"Choose a job that is compatible with being able to raise children/a family. This is a burden that should be placed on both partners in a relationship rather than one woman. It's not inherently harmful, since it is an important career consideration, but I think that conversation shouldn't be exclusive to women."

—Courtney, millennial, engineer

Again, there are plenty of anecdotal stories that show men doing this too. However, research shows us that women are far more likely to feel the pressure to balance both work and home life.

This Kaleidoscope Method is, in some ways, ideal. We all want it all, right? But in reality, this general approach toward work, and what it really means to us as women, renders us so busy trying to blend all the facets of our lives together that we miss the opportunity to self-actualize our goals.

In other words, by trying to keep our lives in balance, we're missing the forest for the trees.

Challenges, Accepted

None of this is to say that women don't work hard, take risks, or excel in their careers. Studies show that women are often the first to accept challenges at work and are motivated by making a real impact at the organization when taking on extra work and hours.

This is where my story about Michelle comes into more focus. Michelle was a perfect example of someone who took on more and more in the hopes that those successes would speak for themselves. That's an approach that assumes far too much of the people around you. You may have the nicest boss, the best team, or the most amazing sponsor, but it's more than that. In my conversations with women over the years, there is a clear disconnect among them in how they perceive the real meaning of working "hard," especially when it comes to alignment with their boss. Oftentimes women don't ask and then end up confusing effort with effectiveness or delivering on their bosses' expectations. Like Michelle, they are focused on checking off as many boxes as they can and overwhelmed with the appearance of "having it all," which we will talk about in the next section.

The truth of the matter is that "hard work" is subjective, and this creates a dilemma for women. Have you ever watched someone rise through your organization's ranks with lower performance than you or your peers? Have you lost out on business because the deal took place in a venue you either didn't have access to or didn't know existed? Have you ever been disappointed that you didn't get the promotion or raise you were expecting after all your sacrifices to help your boss or company succeed? I found it can be confusing.

"Candace, it's great that you're exceeding your goals, and your

team loves you. But unless this leader endorses you, the promotion is a nonstarter. You have to find a way to deliver for his department too, so that he notices your work and will back up your promotion in the talent review."

In my TEDx Talk, I advise women to get on the same page as their boss about their performance. Many women are reaping the rewards for the efforts they make in their job and with their businesses. Some women have accepted that their hard work alone doesn't necessarily speak for itself and is only one of the components needed to have a successful career.

So yes, you must perform well. But the hardest workers I know are also doing these things, which set themselves up for success beyond just the workday:

- **Know how your boss defines hard work.** Don't miss out on this critical first step. Have candid, honest conversations around values, work ethic, and how you can consistently obtain feedback for your performance.

- **Deliver on what is expected.** Most of us love going the extra mile. However, you must deliver on the basic requirements first. Demonstrate that you can do what is expected instead of just trying to "wow" someone with bells and whistles.

- **Ask for help.** You're not going to know everything, and that's okay. Even the president of the United States has a team of advisors. Ask for help when you need it.

- **Develop soft skills.** Your technical skills will only take you so far. You need social and emotional intelligence to work effectively in teams and fit in with the company culture.

- **Have a plan B.** Even the best-thought-out plans can be interrupted for a multitude of reasons. Be sure that you have an action plan for how you'll manage your career in case life—either personal or professional—has some unforeseen surprises in store.

- **Communicate your expectations.** If you take nothing else from this chapter, take this. Your boss is not a mind reader. Tell him or her exactly where you see yourself at the company, and that you expect them to help you get there through their leadership.

You can't have it all . . . or can you?

Facebook COO Sheryl Sandberg is known for bringing topics like feminism, work-life balance, and career-family conflict into pop-cultural conversation. Sandberg's Lean In organization has created unique informal mentoring and networking groups to support working women. In her book *Lean In*, she states:

"Instead of pondering the question, 'Can we have it all?' we should be asking the more practical question, 'Can we do it all?' And again, the answer is no. We often make choices about where we spend our time—between work and family, exercising and relaxing, making time for others and taking time for ourselves."[13]

This is true for millennials as well as older women, and it has been going on for a while. *Time*[14] and *Atlantic Monthly*[15] articles confront this issue, further highlighting the challenges millennial women face. While women of all ages are confronted by difficult workloads, researchers point out that millennials deal with added challenges of being perceived as "complainers" as opposed to their older colleagues, or worse, "not working hard enough."

We would all be wise to take a step back and acknowledge that, while we share a lot of the same challenges as women in the work-

---

13 Sandberg, S. (2013). *Lean in: Women, work, and the will to lead.* Alfred A. Knopf.

14 Slaughter, A. (2012). Why women still can't have it all. *The Atlantic.* http://www. theatlantic. com/magazine/archive/2012/07/why-women-still-cant-have-it-all/309020/

15 Sandler, L. (2013). Having it all without having children. *Time.* http://content.time. com/time/magazine/article/0,9171,2148636,00.html

force, generational differences lead to some intense variations in our experiences, with self-sufficiency and burnout at the top of the list. Millennial women highly value self-sufficiency. Millennial women are more educated, make up more of the workforce, and are more likely to postpone marriage than their grandparents' generation. All these factors interconnect within the sociocultural contexts of inflated metropolitan housing markets and massive student debt. Faced with "surviving" these challenges, many millennial women choose to deprioritize things like self-care and prioritize mental health.

In other words, it's tough out there. If you're a woman who's anxious to make your mark in your career and enjoy the personal life you've always wanted, be prepared to do the following:

- **Accept trade-offs that need to be made.** You might have a well-intentioned boss who tells you you'll be working forty hours a week, but sometimes that won't be the case. Maybe it will be more. Maybe less. Maybe you'll have to sacrifice weekends or holidays, or maybe you'll be asked to pick up slack for whatever reason.

- **Focus on being effective instead of just productive.** Time is always of the essence. Prioritization is key. Work smarter, not longer or harder.

- **Get above petty office politics.** As long as human beings remain social creatures, idle chatter and jockeying for a winning position will never go away. However, while they might be a natural part of business, don't allow yourself to get distracted by gossip or office politics. Be informed, but not absorbed. Gossip and drama are not serving you or your career. You don't have time for it, anyway.

- **Get out of your own way.** Trust me, walking into a meeting assuming or projecting that you are the smartest person in the room isn't doing you any favors. So many successful CEOs are the ones who are humble enough to know that they have plenty to learn from every project and every team member.

- **Make your mental and physical health a priority.** I know it's hard when we all have so much on our plates, but even starting with a few minutes of exercise a day can do wonders for your physical and mental health. Take care of yourself—no one is going to do it for you. Remember to reward yourself too, instead of just those people around you.

- **Make sure you have the support of your significant others.** Healthy relationships include open communication and compromise. If your home life is in chaos because your loved ones are conflicted by your career or business choices, no one is happy.

Your Hard Work Career Zone: Where are you now?

As with the first step in the SHAPE model, getting into the Green Career Zone Behaviors when it comes to hard work will be a work in progress.

Before we look at the chart to get into the Green Career Zone, be sure to do the following:

- **Set a goal and stick to your plan.** For example, if you have not had a formal review with your boss in over a year, set a date for that within the next week. Perhaps you give yourself until the end of the month to evaluate what the next step in your career path should look like.

- **Discuss.** Go beyond simply requesting a review. Set time with your current boss or even the boss of the role you're hoping to get and have a candid discussion about how to get you there.

- **Seek advice.** Build your own internal advisory board or brain trust of people you're confident you can ask for help. Similarly, be a trusted resource for others.

- **Create a plan.** Constantly ask for clarity or inquire if you have missed anything. Understand how you will be evaluated before jumping into your next project. Be 100 percent clear about expectations, always.

- **Business owner? Assess your processes.** Are you using your time wisely? Consider conducting a time and motion study or business efficiency study to ensure the time you and your team are spending on certain tasks is appropriate for the outcomes you are seeking.

- **Do you manage other people?** Be sure you are communicating with your team clearly about what you expect of them.

- **Avoid burnout.** We'll be discussing this in more detail later in the book, but working hard doesn't always mean working endless hours on little to no sleep. Make your mental and physical health a priority.

- **Create clear boundaries.** Healthy boundaries are one of the main components of self-efficacy. Don't ever apologize for prioritizing what matters to you.

- **Forgive yourself for past mistakes.** Use mistakes as learning opportunities and building blocks from which to grow. Avoid letting your past self limit your future. It's okay to be human, own your mistakes, learn from them, and move on.

We will be talking much more about knowing your self-worth throughout this book, and advocating for yourself in the next chapter. As you read the next chart, consider where you are in the framework and how you can start planning to move forward from what's holding you back and celebrate your progress. The colors Red, Yellow, and Green are visual indicators that you are moving in the right path toward strengthening your self-efficacy and building a mindset to position yourself for the career you want and deserve.

Career Zone Assessment: Hard Work

Red Career Zone	Yellow Career Zone	Green Career Zone
• I am overwhelmed at work. • I am afraid to ask for help. • My fear of failure holds me back. • I've been told that I have a poor attitude and work ethic. • I resist being part of company culture. • I blame others for my mistakes. • I am reactive and defensive. • I am burned out. • I am not interested in taking on any more work. • I say things like, "We do this my way or not at all."	• I have a support network I can ask for help. • I can have an open and constructive conversation with my boss about my performance. • I pay attention to the important details in work projects. • Peers recognize me as accountable and easy to work with. • I ask for new opportunities. • I let go of perfectionism. • I solve problems rather than create them. • I take vacations. • I am satisfied with my performance ratings. • I have and manage my boundaries.	• My boss and I are on the same page about my performance. • I regularly exceed expectations. • I am well prepared for meetings and projects. • I have regular meetings with managers and teammates. • I seek and give feedback regularly. • I prioritize self-care. • I am aligned with family and/or spouse. • I don't fear change. • I can use resources to help me make the most efficient and effective use of my time.

KEY CHAPTER TAKEAWAYS:

- Self-efficacy can be diminished if you and the person evaluating your performance are not on the same page. Be aligned with your boss. Women have unique challenges in the workplace—know and understand them, and make choices without apology based on your unique situation.

- Focus on working smarter, not harder.

- You will find that people who don't like, understand, or respect your well-thought-out choices will project their fears onto you. They may even try to make you feel bad for staying at home to raise your kids, pursuing your career, or starting your business. See it for what it is—*their issue, not yours.*

- Be clear about your priorities and the trade-offs you are willing to make for your family. It is okay to choose your family.

- If you are a business owner, have a support network in place to help you navigate your decisions and how you spend your time.

Questions for Further Discussion with Your Support Circle

The components that make up hard work can be subjective and vary by role and industry. Again, this is where your support circle will really be instrumental to your growth. Sometimes, if you want to broaden your point of view, it helps to learn what others are facing. We could certainly spend a lot of time talking about all the ways in which women face challenges in the workplace! Below are questions to help guide a group discussion. It might also be helpful if you include people you have managed and people with a background in human resources. Have a conversation, be open to new ideas and suggestions, and don't forget to download the accompanying workbook to help keep you accountable.

What She Said . . . Reflections from Women

Sometimes it can be difficult to begin a discussion about expectations related to working hard vs. working smart. Below is a series of responses from the women in my study related to their concepts of hard work.

Do any of these statements ring true for you? Why or why not?

- *Work super-long hours to prove you are a team player.*

- *Do anything the boss asks. No matter what it is.*

- *Career advice for women is to just go out there and apply yourself and prove your worth.*

- *Smile more, it could help you out.*

- *If you can dream it, you can be it.*

- *Being told to keep going and keep working hard when that's what you have been doing and no one takes notice of your hard work.*

Additional Questions to Consider:

- Are you and the person who evaluates your performance on the same page about your results? How do you know?

- In what ways do work-life balance, family labor, and hard work interconnect for professional women?

- How do the concepts of work ethic and hard work differ for entrepreneurs?

- What are effective ways to build a brain trust to help expand knowledge gaps?

- Should Gen Z and millennial women be assessed separately from other age groups?

- Would creating faculty and employer roundtables on work-life balance strategies and tips for managing a career, a home life, and common challenges typically met in the first ten to fifteen years of a career be beneficial for assessing women's ideas of hard work?

- How can leaders reconcile driving for performance and limiting burnout?

- How do you help mentor other women who may be overwhelmed at work or with their business?

- If you are a business owner, how are you making sure that you have created an environment where your employees feel comfortable sharing their goals with you?

- How can you help facilitate situations where people can share their life experiences and network with colleagues and peers in a different generation than them?

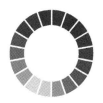

CHAPTER 3:
ADVOCATE FOR YOURSELF SO YOU ARE NOT THE ONE HOLDING YOUR CAREER BACK

"Neither I nor any other females in my generation ever received any advice other than 'be deferential to men.'"

—Susan, baby boomer, administrator

The A in the SHAPE framework is for *Advocate*. Through each of the studies supporting my research for this book, women discussed the importance of speaking up for themselves. The study participants often lamented how dejected they felt when they allowed opportunities to pass them by or the negative impact they felt when they chose to silence themselves. Helplessness has a poor effect on self-efficacy, so it is crucial to find and use your voice.

One of my favorite peers is a woman who has, for the life of her career, been on the CEO trajectory. She is confident, smart, caring, and amazingly driven. No matter the setbacks life has thrown her way, she has achieved incredible success and earned respect and admiration from everyone she's worked with.

She called me one afternoon to share good news: the path to becoming CEO was opening up in front of her. She knew that, soon, she'd be on the short list for the most powerful position at the company. It was the moment she had been working toward her entire life. She had a crucial meeting coming up where she would have the opportunity to put her hat in the ring.

To my shock, I heard hesitation in her voice. When I asked her what was going on, she said simply, "I don't know, Candace. I'm not sure that I'm ready for this!"

I couldn't believe it. If there was one person in the world who was ready for advancement, it was her. But in that moment, she was crippled with self-doubt. Her boss was considering her for the role, yet she wondered if, maybe, she would fail—then what would become of her? Maybe there were other people more qualified, who had done more to position themselves to be next in line for CEO.

I asked her what the job entailed. If she were expected to do the listed tasks as part of her current role, could she do them? Her answer was yes to each question. "You are ready," I challenged her, reminding her that not only was she qualified to be CEO—if she were a man, research showed she likely would not be questioning her "readiness" for the job. After this, I took a moment to reflect on what was really going on in this situation.

It is important to set ourselves up for success financially, which we talked about in chapter 1. It is important to work hard, which we talked about in chapter 2. And it is supremely important that, while we do those things, we continually advocate for ourselves, which we will discuss in this chapter. Self-advocacy is important not just for day-to-day successes, but for paving the path we see ourselves on in future months and years.

When I speak to groups of women, I often lead with a simple question:

"How many of you want to advance in your career?"

Without fail, every hand in the audience goes up.

Then I ask, "How many of you have discussed your career goals with your boss? And are you clear with your boss on exactly how they can help you advance in your career?"

Most hands sheepishly go down when I ask that question. For me, this is incredibly revealing. It tells me that even with all the advances women have made in the workplace, we are still missing this fundamental piece of the puzzle: the skills or assertiveness to advocate for exactly what we want.

I have learned in many cases that it isn't enough to say, "I want a position here." This is an opportunity for clarity, passion, and tenacity. The next time a position opens, push yourself to be clear that you want it. You need to be willing to take the steps and accept the trade-offs necessary to make it happen. And you need to be sure that the key decision-makers know exactly what your intentions are, how you can continually add value, and what you need from them to help you get there.

I am often asked at group events about moments when I felt powerless to speak up in meetings. In truth, I do have doubts on occasion. It's tough being the only woman or sole person of color in the room. Even with my sparkling personality, I know that unfortunately, my presence is not always welcomed. In those moments, I remind myself that I earned my seat at this table and push myself to speak up anyway, especially when inner doubts surface and attempt to compel me to stay silent. I tell myself, You can do this. And if I am afraid, I pray and reach out to my inner circle for strength.

I am also fortunate in that at the beginning of my career, my mentor challenged me to take risks. I've had lots of practice in getting my thoughts past silence or whispers and speaking up on my point of view. If speaking up or speaking out is new or challenging for you, I encourage you to try. Even baby steps are a path forward. And if you find yourself in a place where your voice can't be heard, consider whether you are in the best place for you—and do something about it.

Once, I was asked to consider that perhaps the reason women don't get promotions is that they are not qualified. "That may be the case," I replied. "The trouble I have with this blanket statement, however, is that many times women are not told the truth about their readiness to rise." These women are strung along by their bosses' lack of courage to tell it to them straight, or a manager's inability to develop them so that they can achieve more.

So, ladies, ask for help. Try something different. Remove yourself from harm's way.

Making your voice heard isn't work that happens once a position becomes available at the company or when you are in a meeting. It doesn't happen every now and then when push comes to shove. Advocating for ourselves in the workplace should be a daily practice. The more we advocate for ourselves and others, the less we will find ourselves questioning our "readiness" for the opportunities that arise.

Find Your Voice

In my TEDx Talk, I advise women to speak up for themselves and never choose to silence themselves. Research shows us that generally, women have a harder time speaking up for ourselves than men. Women with families especially are more likely to be risk averse and to employ intentional invisibility as a strategy for navigating workplace barriers. It's a combination of a few things, but I think it can be accurately summed up like this: As a society, women who are compliant are viewed more positively than women who aren't compliant. Women are taught at a young age, through either words or example, that by speaking up for themselves they are being "difficult." Therefore, we learn not to speak up unless we are certain we are right and/or safe.

You know who's not doing all that second-guessing? Your male counterparts.

Which means that no matter how much saving you're doing and how much hard work you're putting in, if you're not advocating for yourself and your future, you are lowering your ability to achieve the success you deserve.

To be sure, women have gotten better at this, especially in recent history. I would never discount all the progress we have made. But we have a way to go, and it starts with you finding your voice, in big and small ways, on a consistent basis.

Some of the best advice ever given to me came early in my career, when I left a meeting filled with basic questions I hadn't asked for fear of looking stupid in front of my new colleagues. I spoke to a mentor about how I was feeling, and his words of wisdom have remained with me ever since.

"Candace, if something isn't clear to you in a meeting, chances are that at least one or two other people in the room have the same question you do. And even if they don't, a little repetition of key concepts or ideas never hurt anyone. Speak up!"

I'm not suggesting you speak up just for the sake of talking during every meeting. But when you believe you have valuable information to share, have a question to pose, or hear something that's unclear to you, don't hesitate to ask for clarification, no matter who is leading the meeting or who might hear your question.

You might be thinking that this sounds good in theory, but in practice can be very intimidating. You're right! If you're the type of person who has never spoken up for herself, it's scary to think that you might need to start, and in the beginning things can be difficult.

And before we go on any further, I'll stop and address an elephant in the room. **Women tend to be looked down upon for asserting themselves or negotiating on their own behalf.** In one laboratory experiment, for example, data revealed that males dislike females who negotiate.[16] Moreover, women who are perceived as displaying anti-stereotypical (aka more aggressive, male-centric) behavior in the workplace are often accused of exhibiting poor social skills. The performance of those women is then evaluated lower.[17,18,19]

Don't let this information dishearten you. In fact, it's all the more reason to be intentional in the ways you assert yourself at work. Knowing different strategies for advocacy and self-efficacy means that you will have a better shot at overcoming gender stereotypes and expectations.

Whether you are a seasoned employee or just starting out in your career, trying your hand at advocating for yourself in big and small ways looks something like this:

- **Requesting a raise.** I'm amazed at how many women complain about how little they are paid, but don't do the simple work of requesting more money for their efforts.

- **Telling your boss your ambitions.** No one is a mind reader. If you have intentions of getting a specific promotion, learning a specific skill, or being considered for a certain position in or out of the company, make sure your boss knows.

- **Stating how you intend to provide value.** It's not enough to simply state that you want a job or role on a project—state

16 Bowles, H. R., Babcock, L., & Lai, L. (2007). Social incentives for sex differences in the propensity to initiate negotiation: Sometimes it does hurt to ask. *Organizational Behavior and Human Decision Processes, 103*, 84–103.

17 Phelan, J. E., Moss-Racusin, C. A., & Rudman, L. A. (2008). Competent yet out in the cold: Shifting criteria for hiring reflect backlash toward agentic women. *Psychology of Women Quarterly, 32*(4), 406–413.

18 Schmader, T., & Johns, M. (2003). Converging evidence that stereotype threat reduces working memory capacity. *Journal of Personality and Social Psychology, 85*, 440–452.

19 Sanchez, C. (2017). Negotiate like a pro to get what you want. *Forbes.* https://www. forbes. com/sites/yec/2017/06/01/negotiate-like-a-pro-to-get-what-you-want/?sh=3f5093097468

why *you* are the perfect person for it. How, specifically, will you add value to the company in that role?

- **Listening to feedback.** Advocating for yourself isn't always about talking—it's also about listening. When your boss tells you what you need to do to earn that pay raise or promotion, take them seriously.

- **Negotiating for what you want.** Although it might feel risky to engage in a negotiation with your boss for any reason, it is essential to develop good negotiation skills in the workplace. Don't think about it in terms of ultimatums—think about it in terms of setting and articulating clear boundaries. For example, if you are negotiating for a bonus on a project and are met with resistance, think about how you can quantify what you've been offered with what is being expected of you.[20]

- **Standing up for yourself.** Workplace bullying is a real thing, and anyone who's been on the receiving end can attest to its damage to morale and performance. Whether it's a new situation or something that's been going on for years, learning to stand up for yourself when others are trying to tear you down is a key part of developing self-efficacy skills.

- **Sharing your contributions/accomplishments.** As women, we are often conditioned to think that talking about our accomplishments makes us arrogant and unlikeable. There is a fine line between bragging and making sure your contributions are seen and celebrated. Meredith Fineman's book *Brag Better* is a great resource for women who are looking for tools to help them become more comfortable with self-promotion.

---

20 For more helpful tips, visit https://time.com/38796/6-hostage-negotiation-techniques-that-will-get-you-what-you-want/

- **Making a business case.** When you're devoted to your work, it's hard not to take things personally when projects don't go your way or you feel as if your suggestions aren't being fully considered. It is always a good idea to "build a business case" for your ideas. Show—specifically—how your suggestion will be good for the company, project, or team. Lead with facts instead of emotion.

- **Forgiving yourself for past mistakes.** This can be tough. Admitting when we've made mistakes and forgiving ourselves for them takes a healthy dose of self-reflection and humility. Choose to reflect on your mistakes and lessons, own up to them, and move past them. Think of them like pearl necklaces whose components were forged over time rather than an albatross around your neck to hold or slow you down.

When it comes to most things, practice makes perfect. Believing in and speaking up for yourself are no exception. The more you practice these skills, the better you'll become.

Creating an Advocacy Network

Advocacy work doesn't begin and end with your personal experience. Once you get comfortable speaking up for yourself when you have an idea you want to share or a concept you want clarified, then we get to the good stuff: building a network of advocates around you.

In my mentorship work, people often ask me, "What is the best way for me to onboard at a new company?" The expected answer usually involves a checklist of some kind. However, my first suggestion is actually centered on creating a network of people who know the quality of your work, know your career aspirations and intentions, and will go to bat for you when needed and support you through difficult times.

If you're thinking this isn't something you can accomplish in the first week on the job, you're right. This is ongoing work, but it's worth it!

Building your advocacy network starts by:

- Being curious and open to learn from others
- Being willing to step outside your comfort zone and tell people about yourself
- Noticing who the decision-makers are on your team and in your larger organization
- Noticing who the most agreeable team players are
- Noticing who the most disagreeable contrarians are
- Making a plan to connect with one or more people from each of those categories

What do I mean by connect? Well, a few things. I mean:

- Setting up one-on-one meetings and talking openly with your potential advocates about your role, your experiences, and your hopes for the future
- Making yourself available to them for consultation and collaboration
- Putting yourself out there by attending team builders or happy hours to make a more personal connection
- Stating directly that you would like them to be your advocate
- Stating directly how you would like them to advocate for you
- Offering yourself as an advocate for them, based on their career goals and aspirations

Again, this is not work that will happen overnight. It will happen through careful planning and prioritization, as well as trial and error. It will happen through quick chats in passing in the hallway, as well as crucial conversations that involve giving and receiving difficult feedback. You'll build your advocacy network by saying things like:

- *I see myself in _____ role in five years, and I would love your guidance.*
- *Will you help me grow in [insert job skill here]?*
- *I want to add more value to this team by _____ . Here's what I need from you to do that.*
- *How can I help you achieve your career goals [e.g., project, department, career]?*
- *I believe I'm ready to take the next step. What do I need to do?*
- *I will launch my business next year. Can I count on you for support?*
- *I want to be a better advocate for myself. Will you help me practice?*

See why finding your voice is so critical?

Putting yourself out there in this way can feel big and scary if you aren't used to asking questions and making bold statements. And here's why it helps: the next time a promotion or business opportunity that you would be right for comes along, you will have a team of people from all different facets of the organization who know not only your work ethic, but what your goals are. You won't have to worry about being at the right meeting and saying the right thing at the right time. You'll have a team of people with whom you have cultivated meaningful relationships who will speak up for you.

And you, in turn, will do the same thing for them. Networks aren't created for just one person's advancement. Building a mutually beneficial advocacy network is a winning strategy across the board. Think of it as building bridges with your peers that you can rely on for the lifetime of your career.

Bridging Generational Communications

In the introduction of this book, I mentioned that I started to notice communications gaps among baby boomers and millennials at work. About fifteen years ago, a leader called an emergency meeting with me. As he sat down in a chair in my office, I was expecting that he wanted to discuss public relations strategies about a critical product launch on the horizon. Instead, he passionately went on and on about the challenges he was having communicating with his team. "I keep telling them exactly what I need them to do, and instead of doing what I say, they keep asking questions and pushing back!" he said.

A few weeks later, another leader called me with a similar refrain—a communications issue had emerged among the younger team members and those most senior, with the younger employees frustrated at what they perceived as older employees throwing meetings and paper trails at a problem that could easily have been solved digitally. About a month after that, one of my mentees shared with me that her patience was being pushed to the limit with all the "out-of-touch leaders" who didn't understand how to use the latest technology and, worse yet, all the time they were wasting. Before I knew it, a considerable amount of my time was being spent counseling leaders on intergenerational communications strategies.

As a communications executive, I often reflect on why and how people speak and interact, particularly when it comes to interpersonal communications, which refers to the way in which people exchange information, feelings, and meaning. We do this through verbal and nonverbal messaging and cues. When we communicate poorly, the outcome can negatively impact what we were trying to achieve and how we feel about our abilities and perceive our future success.

In preparing for this book, I conducted a study on women in the workplace. I wanted to understand which aspects of interpersonal communications resonated among baby boomer, Generation X, millennial, and Generation Z women.

Are you listening?

Adults spend about 70 percent of their waking time communicating.[21] Of this, some 30 percent of communication time is spent speaking, 16 percent reading, and 9 percent writing. A total of 45 percent is spent listening.

From among 1,400 US study participants, I found that female baby boomers believe they are most effective at "Paying attention to others." It's easy to think that communication only relates to how you speak to others. That's part of it, but crucial to speaking is listening.

Some practical ways to show active listening include asking questions or paraphrasing what you've heard. Nonverbal cues such as making eye contact or not looking at your mobile device when someone is speaking to you avoid projecting distraction.

Are you a team player?

I also discovered that Gen X females believe they are most effective at "Working with others."

Some effective ways to demonstrate collaboration are establishing clear goals and expectations, being accountable for the team and yourself, and providing and being open to feedback. It also helps to summarize meetings in writing, so everyone knows what to expect. Being aligned on roles and responsibilities with the other members of the team and making sure there is agreement on the best channels for communication are additional steps you can take.

Are you empathetic?

Both millennials and Gen Z responded that they are most effective at "Showing understanding for others." An effective way to demonstrate empathy is to listen without judging or forming an opinion, be slow to criticize, and acknowledge the other person's feelings as valid for them.

---

21 Adler, R. B., Elmhorst, J., & Lucas, K. (2012). *Communicating at work: Strategies for success in business and the professions* (11th ed.). McGraw-Hill.

Being open to our coworkers' differing values and goals can help us understand and respond to their concerns more effectively.

While we may have a different background and life experience from our colleagues, we can acknowledge others' needs and values without having to apologize for our own. We're all in this together. By focusing on enhancing communication, we can find ways to bring out the best in ourselves and have better interactions at work.

What does this mean for you? It means that as you navigate your career path, create relationships, and work in teams, you will undoubtedly be most effective if you keep any generational differences you might have with the people around you in mind.

It might feel like this is a whole lot to have to take into consideration, all while having to juggle deadlines, your home life, and your future goals. "Candace," I hear people say. "This is too much. I'm just trying to keep my head above water!"

The good news is that any work you put toward effective communication with your peers will pay off in the long run.

Some general tips for effective interpersonal communication are:

- **Practice active listening.** No matter what generation you fall in, looking at your phone or being otherwise distracted while someone is speaking with you is rude and off-putting. Ask questions. Get in the habit of repeating what you've heard.

- **Watch for nonverbal cues.** Experts report that 70 to 90 percent of our communication is nonverbal. Watch for crossed arms or clenched jaws. Be carefully attentive to the "energy" that the person/people you are working with give off.

- **Establish clear goals and expectations.** Whether it's your weekly staff meeting, a one-on-one with your boss, or a team collaboration, it's always good to get in the habit of starting off by making your goals clear. Summarize important meetings in writing.

- **Make sure everyone is aligned on roles and responsibilities.** Again, this is important whether you're a business owner with a team of two or an individual contributor at a company with thousands of employees. Everyone, no matter their generational context, will appreciate knowing exactly what they are accountable for.

- **Establish rules for communication.** One of the biggest ways our generational differences play out is in styles of communication. If your baby boomer colleague prefers a phone call, pick up the phone and have a conversation. If your Gen X boss needs things written in an email, do that. If you are managing a team of millennials that prefer texting, find a way to make it so your team is communicating effectively in that way.

- **Put yourself in someone else's shoes.** In my study, both millennials and Gen Z responded that they feel they are most effective at "Showing understanding of others." This is a good thing. It means the key to building effective work relationships includes showing empathy. Think about it this way: you want people to understand your point of view, right? Start by showing others the same courtesy. Avoid being quick to judge people of a different generation for the ways in which they process information, manage stress, or communicate.

Effective Negotiation

While all this might sound doable in theory, there is no doubt that in practice learning to find and consistently use your voice can be a challenge. Inspiration can come from anywhere. Early in my career, while reading an in-flight magazine seminar ad on negotiation, I read a quote by negotiation expert Dr. Chester Karris: *"In business as in life, you don't get what you deserve, you get what you negotiate."*

The art of negotiation is a powerful skill to master in your career.

I learned this quickly. Early in my career, over lunch a colleague complained about his salary. Outwardly calm as I sat across from him, I was internally shocked. He was making quite a bit more money per year than I was. When I say "quite a bit," I mean 35 percent more than I was. Not only that, but my sales numbers were ten times higher than his. In other words, I was earning ten times more profit for the company and getting paid 35 percent less.

Of course, I was angry and hurt when I learned the news, especially considering how disappointed my colleague felt that he was so underpaid. I had to address it. But I knew that leading with emotion was not the way to get what I wanted and deserved. I wanted to have a business conversation.

After scheduling a meeting with the leader of my department, I came in prepared. I clearly discussed my sustained financial and staff development contributions to the company. I let her know that I wanted my compensation to match my contribution, full stop—and that knowing it didn't was demotivating for me. I told her that I enjoyed working for the company and wanted to stay, but that I, like her, was contacted by recruiters all the time. If she couldn't pay me what I knew I deserved and had earned, those offers might be more tempting. I shared with her that I'd noticed women in our profession tend to age out in their early fifties; I was in my prime earning years and needed to set myself up well now for retirement.

The stark reality is that many women are taught, by either word or example, that the best strategy for doing well at work (i.e., providing value) is to keep their heads down and get things done, avoiding anyone and anything that might get in the way of the product they are producing. Additionally, because women tend to be more conflict-averse than their male counterparts, workplace bullies often see them as easy targets. Women tend to carry the trauma from being bullied in the workplace well into our careers.[22]

22 Reuell, P. (2016). Resolving conflict: Men vs. women. *Harvard Gazette*. https://news.harvard.edu/gazette/story/2016/08/resolving-conflict-men-vs-women/.

When we are in difficult workplace situations, it's easy to allow challenges to affect our performance and overall happiness at the company. I have been in this situation more than once. It's not easy to find your voice and be confident in yourself when you're dealing with a strained interpersonal relationship with a boss or coworker. This is where working to understand our generational and cultural difference is crucial. You must get to the root of the issue to correct it.

Again, easier said than done. But in my experience, all the work you do to find your voice as an advocate for yourself and form a team of people to back you up when times are tough will become especially important here.

How many times have you heard women around you say, "Fine. I'll make it work"? Approaching your career with the attitude that someone else is in control is a great way to build disappointment, resentment, and disillusionment.

"What is getting in the way of our communication?" I might say to someone I'm in conflict with. "Here's what I'm willing to do to repair this relationship, and this is what I need from you."

If this feels too hard, too confrontational, or too uncomfortable, I want you to remember this:

Suffering in silence isn't helping you. It will erode much of the work you've done toward boosting your self-efficacy. If you want to advance your career, you must find your voice and use it, even when it seems scary or difficult.

So, where do you begin to put your self-efficacy into practice when you're in a challenging spot?

No matter the situation, start with listing your nonnegotiables. Maybe your list includes a health care package as part of your compensation, a certain base salary, or a specific dollar amount for a project you are tasked to complete. Do your homework and be clear about the things you simply cannot and will not bend on.

When you're in negotiations, try not to shy away from difficult conversations. Lead with positive elements of your collaboration and find the ways in which you and the person you're in conflict with are in sync. Frame your ask so it's not such a heavy lift for the person you're talking to. When in doubt, check out the myriad articles published on the web that lay out all the different negotiation tactics you can try.

Tips on Negotiating

Many women often tell me how much they hate negotiating—period. They share how engaging in negotiations makes them feel intimidated and helpless. Some just don't want to deal with the rejection.

Sound familiar?

At the same time, women consistently report in my studies that there have been times they haven't negotiated well for a promotion, raise, idea, project, or job, resulting in disappointment and frustration.

Learning how to negotiate for what you want and deserve can certainly feel intimidating, but getting good at this when the stakes are low will set you up for success when the stakes are high. It all involves getting emotionally and mentally ready before a critical discussion.

Here are some tips from experts I often share with my mentees for honing your negotiation skills.

1.   **Draw upon the power of silence**

It is human nature to rush to fill up any uncomfortable silences in conversations, especially if they are high stakes. This, however, can be a mistake. Quiet moments in conversations allow you to fully absorb what your counterpart has just said, both verbally and nonverbally, says Harvard Business School and Harvard Law School professor Guhan Subramanian. This is even more important if your counterpart has suggested a resolution to your conflict that is outrageous or unacceptable to you. "Your stunned silence will far more effectively defuse the anchor than heaps of protesting would," says Subramanian.[23]

23 Shonk, K. (2020). *5 Good Negotiation Tactics*. Harvard Law School. https://www.pon.harvard.edu/daily/negotiation-skills-daily/5-good-negotiation-techniques/.

2. **Always ask for what you want**

You will never get what you don't ask for. This is especially true for women and people of minority backgrounds—there is much research that proves that we don't negotiate enough. Often, this can be as simple as saying very directly what we want. If we look at salaries alone, it's imperative. In Linda Babcock's book *Women Don't Ask*, she found that about 7 percent of female MBAs tried to negotiate, compared to 57 percent of men from the same program.[24]

3. **Assume you might actually *get* what you want**

Engaging in negotiations with a mindset that the outcome will work in your favor will give you an advantage in many ways. First, it will make you less fearful and more confident in your conversation. Second, you will be more thoughtful in your negotiations. When you assume success, chances are you'll be more thoughtful in creating a win-win situation and not be emotional or reactive.[25]

4. **Do your homework**

Skilled negotiators never come to the table unprepared. Come into conversations with data to back up your feelings and requests. For example, if you're negotiating for your ideal salary, research the industry so you can come to the table with realistic requests and expectations. That way, when you're asked questions and presented with counterarguments, you'll be better prepared to respond and push back, if necessary.

5. **Ask open-ended questions**

24 Babcock, L., & Laschever, S. (2007). *Women don't ask: The high cost of avoiding negotiation—and positive strategies for change.* Bantam.

25 Sanchez, C. (2017). Negotiate like a pro to get what you want. *Forbes.* https://www. forbes. com/sites/yec/2017/06/01/negotiate-like-a-pro-to-get-what-you-want/?sh=3f5093097468

So much of collaborative negotiation relies on trust. Building a trusting relationship involves coming to the table calm and prepared, but it also involves being open to discourse. You don't want to receive simple "yes" or "no" responses—you want the other person to engage with you and be open to understanding your thought process. Do this by asking open-ended questions and focusing on establishing a trusting relationship.[26]

6. **Be prepared to give something up**

We can't talk about negotiation without acknowledging that you are not always going to get everything you want. The trick to being flexible revolves around being able to clearly identify the areas where you're willing to bend and where you're not. For example, if you're negotiating with a vendor, you might be willing to pay more than what you'd ask for because they are offering you something in return that makes that concession worth it. Similarly, if you are negotiating your salary, you may be willing to accept less than you asked for knowing that you will be compensated in other ways that make the agreement fair.[27]

7. **Always seek clarity**

Whenever you are negotiating for something, it is common for misconceptions to occur, since both parties assume what the other person is implying or thinking. (This can happen in general conversations too!) If you are in negotiations and see a confused look on the other person's face or get a sense that there is a conflict brewing, ask them to repeat the deal how they see it. Doing this accomplishes a couple different things: first, it allows you to see the situation from their

---

26 Rampton, J. (2016). *13 Negotiating Techniques That Never Fail.* Inc. https://www.inc.com/john-rampton/13-negotiation-techniques-that-never-fail.html

27 Rampton, J. (2016). *13 Negotiating Techniques That Never Fail.* Inc. https://www.inc.com/john-rampton/13-negotiation-techniques-that-never-fail.html

point of view and clarify any misconceptions.[28] Second, it reinforces the trusting relationship you know will help you close the deal more quickly. The best negotiations end with both parties feeling heard, seen, and understood.[29]

Will you always be successful with your negotiations? No. Remember my discussion earlier in this chapter about my own pay? Despite doing all these things when negotiating my salary all those years ago, I was met with resistance. I didn't get the raise I'd earned or a satisfactory explanation.

So, do you know what I did? I tried one more time and still didn't get the result I wanted. So, I quit, professionally and gracefully. I did my best to advocate for myself, and when it didn't work out, I continued to deliver on my role, activated my network, found another role, and left. I didn't take it personally. I wasn't bitter. I took action.

In fact, I remember that when I left that position, a key leader met with me and said, "I knew you weren't going to make it here."

I looked her in the eyes, smiled, and said, "I am very proud of my accomplishments here." I then listed all of them. "I will take everything I achieved here and apply it to my new role." And that's exactly what I did.

She mistakenly thought that she was going to erode my self-efficacy as a parting gift. *She was wrong.* You may encounter people who try to project their hurt, frustration, and disappointment onto you. Recognize this for what it is and keep moving forward.

Not everyone will champion your success. Hurt people try to hurt people. Let your progress move you in a forward direction.

Fortunately, as time passed, there were many times when my negotiations worked in my favor. And over time my skills got better. In the next chapter, we are going to talk much more about perseverance during

---

28 Barker, R. (2014). 6 Hostage Negotiation Techniques That Will Get You What You Want. *Time.* https://time.com/38796/6-hostage-negotiation-techniques-that-will-get-you-what-you-want/

29 Sanchez, C. (2017). Negotiate like a pro to get what you want. *Forbes.* https://www. forbes. com/sites/yec/2017/06/01/negotiate-like-a-pro-to-get-what-you-want/?sh=3f5093097468

difficult times, but until then I'll remind you that the point of advocating for yourself isn't to win every argument or get your way all the time. It also isn't just about getting people to like you or agree with you.

Self-advocacy is about taking control of your career with intention and leading with integrity. This is important when times are good, but it's especially important when times are hard.

During a farewell lunch, a coworker gave me a curio box that I keep on my desk. Its inscription sums things up perfectly:

"Life isn't about waiting for the storm to pass;
it's about learning to dance in the rain."

—Vivian Greene

I look at this box often and remind myself about the importance of embracing the journey.

Think about how much better your life and career would be if you learned how to do things even when they're hard.

Your Advocacy Career Zone: Where are you now?

It can be hard to know how you are progressing in your path toward self-advocacy, especially as you are first starting out or if you've not done it before. Before we look at the chart to get into the Green Career Zone, be sure to do the following:

- **Speak up**. Easier said than done at times, but the first step to self-advocacy is finding your voice and using it.

- **Do more than the bare minimum**. If you want to be taken seriously when you speak up for yourself, show yourself to be the accomplished contributor that you are! Create a reputation of delivering value.

- **Be open to creating healthy relationships with co-workers**. Oftentimes, advocacy takes a village. Create an advocacy network you can rely on, and be a person who others can rely on too.

- **Be brave when it comes to difficult conversations.** Advocating for yourself can feel scary. Get into the habit of having hard conversations, especially if avoiding these tough moments will breed resentment.

- **Seek out opportunities, even if they seem scary.** You're never going to know what opportunities you have if you don't take the time to seek them out. If there's a job you want, apply for it. If there's a contact you'd love to make, make it!

- **Create your support network.** Knowing when to advocate for yourself doesn't have to feel isolating. Surround yourself with supportive allies and nurture those relationships; you never know when you will need them.

- **If you are a business owner, build healthy alliances in your community.** If you're managing a business, you might not be advocating for yourself to a boss, but you will be advocating for yourself in other ways. Seek out healthy relationships with others to help you through this.

- **If you manage people, be approachable.** If your employees are advocating for themselves at work, recognize that it takes courage and confidence. Be the type of employer who rewards risk-taking.

- **Let go of perfectionism.** Perfectionism is an impossible goal. You won't get this right all the time, and that's okay. (Much more on this in the next chapter.)

- **Be flexible.** Don't be myopic when it comes to advocating for yourself. You know the adage about one door closing and another one opening? It's true if you allow it to be.

As you read the next chart, consider where you are in the framework and how you can start planning to move forward from what's holding you back and celebrate your progress in speaking up for yourself. In the meantime, the colors Red, Yellow, and Green associated with the career zones below are visual indicators that you are moving in the right path toward strengthening your advocacy skills and building a mindset to position yourself for the career you want and deserve.

Career Zone Assessment: Advocacy

Red Career Zone	Yellow Career Zone	Green Career Zone
• I can't speak up. • I avoid conflict. • I am afraid of speaking up. • I do only the bare minimum. • I complain often. • I refuse to have difficult conversations. • I make excuses for why I am passed over for every opportunity. • I avoid conflict. • I don't want to hurt anyone's feelings, so I prefer to say nothing. • I am not prepared for an unexpected response to me speaking up.	• I have a support network I can ask for help. • I can reframe negative self-talk. • I believe I can change my current circumstance. • I can put a plan in place to deal with the ramifications of speaking up. • I take pride in doing tasks well. • I take responsibility for mistakes. • I have begun creating a network of peers to lean on. • I speak up, even when it's challenging. • I am willing to negotiate. • My past doesn't define me.	• I am prepared for the trade-offs and consequences of speaking up. • I've built alliances to help me have a better path to success. • I consistently advocate for myself and others. • I consistently exceed expectations and have clear goals. • I lead by clearly stating how I will provide value. • I listen to and follow advice from people I trust. • I am comfortable with the responsibility of leading others. • I can say "no." • I can deal with rejection. • I will negotiate.

KEY CHAPTER TAKEAWAYS:

- You fortify your self-efficacy when you find your voice and use it consistently. Practice speaking up as often as you can. Start with small things, and when the stakes are high, test out and think through different strategies.

- Speaking up can be risky. You aren't in this alone! Build a support network so you will know which issues to escalate and brainstorm best practices.

- Don't be afraid of having difficult conversations—take risks and speak up for yourself! You will make mistakes—own them and move on. Mistakes are part of life!

- Learn to negotiate and "brag better." You are your own best advocate!

- If you are a business owner, create an environment where your employees feel they can advocate for themselves. If you are an entrepreneur, stay current on the research about your business to be sure that you are being adequately compensated and valued.

Questions for Further Discussion with Your Support Circle

I mention the importance of not going it alone many times throughout this book, but this is especially critical when it comes to learning how to be a good advocate for yourself. Here are some questions for you to take to your discussion group. Have a conversation, be open to new ideas and suggestions, and don't forget to download the accompanying workbook on my website to help keep you accountable.

What She Said . . . Reflections from Women

Sometimes it can be difficult to begin a discussion about finding your voice and speaking up for yourself. You may find strength in numbers via a reading group or support circle. Below is a series of responses from the women in my study related to the concept of advocating for yourself for you to consider and discuss.

Do any of these statements ring true for you? Why or why not?

- *I remember going into my boss's office to ask for a raise and being told, "I can't afford to give you that kind of raise or I'll be out of business." My thought was that if I'm that good, I can give you the kind of money to make you more profits.*

- *There is this idea of fairness and that men and women are promoted only on their merits. Harmful because women will believe it.*

- *Don't ask too many questions.*

- *The boss is always right.*

- *Keep your head down and do what's asked.*

- *Never complain.*

- *"Do not try to get paid what a man would. Just accept whatever salary you get." This is not fair; you should be paid for your skill, not your gender.*

- *I can only speak for myself, but I was told not to be so ambitious and to be satisfied with what I had.*

- *People need to be taught to stand up for themselves. Women are trained to be accommodating. They need to learn to advocate for themselves.*

Additional Questions to Consider:

- How do you decide when it is best to speak up and when it is best to be silent?

- Can you point to a time in your career when you didn't advocate for yourself? What happened?

- Can invisibility be an effective strategy for women, especially those less interested in "rocking the boat"?

- What generation do you associate with in terms of your communication style? How does it impact how you communicate with others?

- What are the most effective ways you have negotiated in the past?

- Why do you believe it is difficult for women to advocate for themselves?

- Do you have a sponsor at work? If not, how can you plan to get one?

- Have you ever sponsored others? If not, how can you plan to be a sponsor for someone else?

- If you own your own business, what changes do you think you can make to your environment so your employees feel more comfortable during challenging conversations?

- If you are a solo entrepreneur, how do you evaluate what you spend your time and energy on?

- If you own a small business, how can you best prioritize networking events so you feel supported?

CHAPTER 4:

PERSEVERE TO NAVIGATE YOUR CAREER JOURNEY OVER THE LONG TERM

"Women must be willing and prepared to persevere, because times do get tough. We need support systems, coping mechanisms, and hope."

—Lauren, Gen X, lawyer

The P in the SHAPE framework stands for *Persevere.* When asked what advice women would offer to their younger selves or to women just launching their careers, the study participants provided encouragement to others to not give up. More than ever, the ability to keep going despite hardships or deferred success is front and center. The inability to persevere can feed self-doubt and, in turn, erode your self-efficacy.

━━ ━━ ━━ ▬▬ ▬▬

A former boss would always say, *"Every company is like a microcosm of the world. Everything that happens out there, happens in here. We must be prepared to deal with it when it shows up."* The quote ran through my mind one day as I tried to console a colleague who'd broken down at work over a seemingly minor disagreement with another coworker.

Pam had a secret shame. Something had happened to her that should never happen to a woman: she was assaulted by someone she believed she could trust. When that happened, something inside her broke. As the years passed, she mastered hiding the shame from others, but it stayed with her, and occasionally she would think about how helpless she'd felt when the assault happened to her. Despite her best efforts, whenever fear would creep into her life, particularly her work life, that same helpless feeling would follow.

It impacted her interactions with her colleagues and her performance at work. Regardless of her academic achievements, criticism from a manager or conflict with a coworker took her back to that difficult, helpless space and paralyzed her mentally and emotionally. This amazing woman would be transported back to a place she never asked to go.

We're going to talk in this chapter about persevering through hard times—knowing when to keep going, knowing when to quit. It's interesting that even though our brains are quite complex, they're very inefficient in how they process pain and trauma. Many times, it's hard for us to differentiate one pain from the trauma of another. Simply put, sometimes we transfer a past hurt onto a present hurt, and the memory sticks. Unresolved past traumas continue to creep back into our lives. Unless we can successfully cope with them, we continue to process and project negative ideas, thoughts, and behaviors that erode our self-efficacy and even show up in our performance at work.

When Pam shared her story with me, I looked at her, thanked her, and expressed my sadness for what had happened. I asked her if she'd ever considered getting help. She replied, *"I don't want to talk about it because I don't want to have to relive it and deal with it."*

As her friend, I told her that I could listen and empathize with her but also reminded her that making a choice to do nothing is also a choice. *"Maybe one day you'll make a choice to get help, but promise me that you won't feel bad about the time it took for you to get there. Just be grateful that you did."*

If you've been a victim of something unspeakable, the first thing I like to remind you is that you're not responsible for what someone did to you that you did not ask for or deserve. Give yourself a gift of time, understanding, and empathy as you make your own journey to resolve what happened to you. I encourage you to treat yourself with love and kindness rather than shame as you make your way through to the other side.

As Pam's story shows, work isn't a vacuum in which we can work without being affected by things from "outside." Our lives aren't divided into neat boxes—and grief can all too easily affect the arc of your career if you're unable to deal with it in a healthy way.

Space to Grieve

Sometimes when I think about the power of perseverance, I think back to my fiancé, Dwayne. After he died, you can imagine I was in a lonely and empty space. I stopped sleeping at night; instead, I stared at the ceiling as I lay in bed and spent countless hours in prayer. I tried to throw myself into work, yet it was difficult. Grief is a powerful thing.

One of my colleagues saw how much I was struggling and pulled me aside. *"Candace,"* she said, *"it's breaking our hearts to see you suffering so much every day. You had such a vibrant energy; now you look exhausted. You're a shell of yourself. You need to rest. I have a friend with a house in the Bahamas, and I reached out to ask her if you could stay with her for a week or so, to catch your breath and relax. I found a cheap ticket for you to leave on Sunday. Please, do.*"

I reached out to my best friend for advice. She looked at me and said, "*Go!*"

My boss was very empathetic. When I went to him and asked how he would feel about me taking an unscheduled vacation, he immediately said, "*Please! Please go!*" He basically shooed me out the door, knowing how important it was that I recharge after such a difficult experience.

My time with my generous host, Beverly, has remained with me all these years. She was sixty-five years old and a kind and lovely woman. On our first night together, she showed me around the island, took me to dinner, and gave me space to rest and grieve. It was exactly the escape I needed at that moment to rest, reflect, and recharge.

On my last night on the island, during dinner I told her that I was scared and didn't know what to do with the rest of my life. In response, she shared her story with me. From my vantage point, Beverly appeared to be living a successful, wonderful life, yet her story revealed something different. She had sacrificed everything—and I mean everything—for her children and her husband. And in the end, they hadn't appreciated everything she had done to make their lives better. They'd abandoned her and refused her gifts. It was truly one of the saddest stories I'd ever heard. And yet with all she'd been through, and all she seemed to have lost, instead of being filled with resentment, she seemed to have made her peace with her life.

As I sat there processing her story, I was inspired. I thanked her for her graciousness and hospitality.

"*Candace,*" she replied, "*the greatest gift I can give you isn't my home to stay in. It's my story. Someday, you'll be sixty-five like me. If you find yourself sitting on the other side of a table from a twenty-five-year-old woman with a broken heart, I want you to tell her how, in spite of all the hardships you've been through already, you've led an amazing life. I want you to focus from here on out on making an amazing life and career for yourself with a story that you will be proud of telling.*"

When I came back from my visit with her, I took a long, hard look at what I wanted my life to look like from that point on. I envisioned the career I wanted, the life I knew I could achieve. I still *could* achieve it, even though I was still dealing with my tragedy.

Before we go into more stories and research, the best advice I can give you is this:

Choose how you want to guide your life and career decisions for yourself.

For me, my guiding star has always been the desire to create an amazing life.

Be your authentic self, always. Be unwilling to compromise on the life you want and deserve. Your journey is your journey. With this as your foundation, perseverance will be much easier.

> *"The advice to play it safe and not get out of your comfort zone because of your gender is more harmful than helpful—not only is it putting you down as a woman, it's not letting you use your full potential."*
>
> *—Jennifer, millennial, nonprofit director*

Hardships and Perseverance

Undoubtedly, like Pam, the hardships you deal with in life will inform how you show up at work. For many women, this takes the form of perfectionism. Because there is little they can control about their current situation, they try to control their work environment. When things go wrong—and they will—they beat themselves up for their mistakes.

If this rings any bells for you, I can promise you are not alone. Getting past this starts with self-awareness.

Surviving hardships shows up in other ways as well. One of my dearest colleagues, Brenda, had a difficult childhood marked by poverty. She desperately wanted to go to college, but she knew her family could never afford it. However, she was not going to let her circumstances stop her. After high school, she took on an administrative position during the day and went to night school. Eventually, her entry-level position turned into a years-long management position. By all accounts, she was an incredible success story.

Even so, there was always something reminding her of where she came from, and not in a good way. Whether it was a snide comment from coworkers about her "secretary" days or a well-intentioned remark about how hard she must have worked to get where she had, Brenda always harbored nagging doubts as to whether she really belonged where she was.

When we spoke about this, she would often put herself down. "It's so stupid," she would say. "I could probably run circles around everyone at the company at this point, but there's always a part of me that doesn't feel good enough."

In my experience, women tend to walk away from difficult situations too soon. Instead of taking on challenges that present themselves, they talk themselves out of being good enough. They let negative self-talk lead them to quit.

What path might Brenda be on if she developed the self-efficacy skills I've described in this book? If she could get past her self-doubt, make it a habit to ask for help, and make sure her goals and desires were heard?

Recommending perseverance, of course, doesn't mean that I would recommend staying miserable. There is a fine line between grudgingly sticking it out because you think you should and finding the courage and wherewithal to overcome challenges.

What I told Brenda that day is what I tell women all the time: All the trials you've gone through, be they poverty, lack of education, loss, illness, or anything else that has forced you to pivot and adapt, have been stepping stones toward one of the most important elements of your career and your life: perseverance.

Believe it or not, you should consider yourself lucky to have gone through those trials! The resilience you earned along the way has undoubtedly made you into the capable leader you are.

Of course, Brenda, or any woman reading this book who can relate to Brenda's story, is going to remember moments when she wrestled with feelings of inadequacy and self-doubt. But before we go into any of the elements of how to make perseverance a consistent part of getting your work life in SHAPE, I want you to remember that you already have the tools you need to persevere. You've gained them simply through working as hard as you have to get where you are.

Now is the time for you to put the tools in this book into action.

"Practice makes perfect? I think practice makes progress.
No one can ever be perfect, that's just the truth."

—*Felicia, Gen X, architect*

Perseverance, Resilience, and Grit

Oftentimes, we use terms interchangeably to define our or others' success. For this book's purposes, though, I want to take some time to talk about what some of these important words mean. That way, when you use them in your own life you can be clear on the next steps on your SHAPE path.

Perseverance: Technically, perseverance is "the continued effort to do or achieve something despite difficulties, failure, or opposition." Perseverance tends to be associated with steadfastness in mastering skills or completing a task—in other words, having a commitment to learning. I focus on perseverance in career coaching because careers are journeys. The average person will have stops and starts along the way. The reasons vary; maybe you want to change roles to take on more growth and increase your income. In fact, a woman might have up to eight to ten jobs during her career! Your ability to get through the ups and downs will be dependent upon your ability to weather storms—your perseverance.

Resilience: When we speak of resilience in a formal way, we mean "an ability to recover from or adjust easily to misfortune or change." Simply put, resilience is the ability to bounce back after adversity or disappointment, to manage and adapt to sources of stress or adversity. Perhaps your role was suddenly eliminated or changed, or you were laid off unexpectedly. Is this difficult? Absolutely! But it's critical when it comes to riding the waves that your career journey will present you.

Grit: In her book *Grit: The Power of Passion and Perseverance*, Angela Duckworth defines the titular term as the tendency to sustain interest and effort toward long-term goals, associated with self-control and deferring short-term gratification. Duckworth has found that grit—a combination of passion and perseverance for a singularly important goal—is the hallmark of high achievers in every domain. Perhaps you have had a setback or have been told the odds are not in your favor, but you still do what it takes to advance your career. I highly recommend her book for much more on her incredible research and findings.

Regardless of the subtle differences in definitions, one thing remains the same: perseverance, resilience, and grit are hard to quantify and highly situational. However, there is plenty of research showing us a few key findings.

1. Individual resilience and organizational resilience are two different things. You can be the most motivated employee in the world, but if your company cannot pivot when times are tough, where does that leave you?[30]

2. Social support and interpersonal relationships are key to

---

30 Branicki, L., Steyer, V., & Sullivan-Taylor, B. (2016). Why resilience managers aren't resilient, and what human resource management can do about it. *The International Journal of Human Resource Management*. http://dx.doi.org/10.1080/09585192.2016.1244104

building a foundation of perseverance and resilience. What can you do if you don't have those important pieces in place?[31,32,33,34,35]

3. Resiliency is often associated with masculinity, be it stoicism or heroic forms of crisis intervention.[36] How does this distinction impact women in the workplace?

The truth is that women do feel the effects of perseverance, resilience, and grit differently. Data show us that women are more likely than men to be in unstable types of employment throughout their lives regardless of educational level; this occurs both early and later in their career, often due to the generational challenges we've highlighted in this book so far.[37]

Simply put, women disproportionately deal with workplace situations where they must demonstrate resilience. Your ability to persevere through hard times is essential to your success.

31 Flach, F. (1997). *Resilience: Discovering a new strength at times of stress.* Fawcett Columbine.

32 Jackson, D., Firtko, A., & Edenborough, M. (2007). Personal resilience as a strategy for surviving and thriving in the face of workplace adversity: A literature review. *Journal of Advanced Nursing, 60*(1), 1–9.

33 Powley, E. H. (2009). Reclaiming resilience and safety: Resilience activation in the critical period of crisis. *Human Relations, 62*(9), 1289–1326.

34 Stephens, J. P., Heaphy, E. D., Carmeli, A., Spreitzer, G. M., & Dutton, J. E. (2013). Relationship quality and virtuousness: Emotional carrying capacity as a source of individual and team resilience. *The Journal of Applied Behavioral Science, 49*, 13–41.

35 Tugade, M. M., & Fredrickson, B. L. (2004). Resilient individuals use positive emotions to bounce back from negative emotional experiences. *Journal of Personality and Social Psychology, 86*(2), 320–333.

36 Branicki, L., Steyer, V., & Sullivan-Taylor, B. (2016). Why resilience managers aren't resilient, and what human resource management can do about it. *The International Journal of Human Resource Management.* http://dx.doi.org/10.1080/09585192.2016.1244104

37 European Institute for Gender Equality. (2017). Gender, skills and precarious work in the EU. Research note. EIGE. http://eige.europa.eu/rdc/eige-publications/genderskills-and-precarious-work-eu-research-note

Persevering as a Small Business Owner

According to an American Express OPEN "The State of Women-Owned Businesses 2019" report, there were about 11.6 million female-owned small businesses in the US that year, and that number is steadily growing.[38] Whether you became an entrepreneur because you were ready to exit corporate life, were eager for a more flexible schedule to be with your children, launched due to the pandemic, or simply felt called to be your own boss, chances are that you know all about the importance of perseverance when it comes to owning and operating your own business.

I have heard women who own small businesses describe feeling under pressure like everyone else, but with the bonus of feeling like they are also under a blinding spotlight. That is because they are assuming all the risks, financial and otherwise, as well as operating in a place of vulnerability, since they might be taking a pay cut as their business (hopefully) grows.

In short, owning your own business isn't for the faint of heart. That's even more reason for you to develop your perseverance skills.

I once worked with a woman who started her own business after staying home with her children for several years after they were born. She was an expert in her field and had thrived in her career before kids. However, it was better for her family that she was able to control her daily schedule, so when it was time to go back to work, she decided to go out on her own.

She considered herself organized, but all it took was one meeting with a small business coach to make her feel like she was in way over her head. Web hosting? Business agreements? Taxes? It all felt so overwhelming to her. Why was she doing this again?

All your work toward building self-efficacy will play a critical role in developing perseverance through hard times as a business owner. You will need to weather the day-to-day ups and downs of running the

38 American Express. (2019). The State of Women-Owned Businesses Report. https://s1.q4cdn. com/692158879/files/doc_library/file/2019-state-of-women-owned-businesses-report.pdf

show, and you'll also need to have the self-confidence and time management skills to prioritize your mental health and your long-term
vision for your company.

When I mentor women who have chosen the path of entrepreneurship, I speak about perseverance in terms of setting clear and
effective boundaries.

- **Avoid burnout.** Do not fall into the trap of working all the
  time. Do your best to keep to a schedule and to keep your
  downtime sacred.

- **Always get paid for your work.** In my experience, women
  often undervalue their work or give away their time for free.
  Volunteering your time intentionally is one thing, but don't
  allow others to take your work for nothing.

- **Be careful mixing business and pleasure.** If you have
  a small business that your friends and family patronize, that
  is great! But be careful allowing boundaries to blur when it
  comes to your time, your cost, or your energy.

- **Prioritize networking.** Owning your own business can
  be wonderful, but also isolating. Make sure you prioritize
  attending events where you can mix with other female entrepreneurs and learn from them.

- **Make time for long-term planning.** So many entrepreneurs feel like it's all they can do to manage their business
  day to day. Hard work is important, but so is stepping back
  and making sure your long-term goals for your company and
  your personal life are on track.

I've spoken with many women over the years who have found the
rewards of owning their own business to be many. They can set their
own schedules, take on more or less work based on their personal life
situation, and feel like they have the "best of both worlds."

I have also spoken with many women who started their own business only to see it fold within a couple years. Often, it has nothing to do with the business itself and everything to do with their ability to get through the many ups and downs of entrepreneurship.

When times are hard as a small business owner, your perseverance is key. No one is guaranteed success—the work you do to build your resilience and grit will always be helpful to you in the long run.

Perseverance Pitfalls

As with so many things, your journey toward the Green Career Zone on the SHAPE path is not one you go through alone. We've already spoken about this in the previous chapter, but it's worth repeating here:

Building a network of people you trust to help you through the ups and downs of your career journey is essential to your long-term advocacy and success.

Why is this so important? Your career journey is going to be filled with moments of self-doubt. Do any of these situations sound familiar?

- **Default on career promissory note:** Sometimes a manager will intentionally dangle the carrot of a raise, promotion, or big opportunity in front of you. You become so focused on achieving the "promised" reward that you eagerly overextend yourself to deliver. When you do deliver, your manager moves the goal line. You double down on your efforts and continue delivering. However, the reward never comes, just excuses and more assignments—never the truth. Sometimes, you may be led to believe that you misinterpreted the "promise," or that circumstances have changed and the terms of your reward are no longer valid—there isn't any recognition beyond keeping your job. If the reward was a key driver for you, a career promissory note default can be devastating, especially if the person who made the promise wasn't forthright. Most people I've met who experience this career promise default leave their roles. Sadly, some managers never fully understand the damage they leave in the wake. The employee loses trust in management (and tells people what happened). Those affected lose face with their support system—who saw the writing on the wall all along. The key here is to not blame yourself and to try to stay levelheaded as you navigate to your more authentic opportunity.

- **Imposter syndrome**: Imposter syndrome is a psychological pattern in which an individual doubts their skills, talents, or accomplishments and has a persistent internalized fear of being exposed as a "fraud." Simply put, imposter syndrome is that constant nagging feeling many of us struggle with that we aren't good enough for our roles. I have seen some of the most successful, outwardly confident women I know struggle with imposter syndrome.

- **The desire to quit when things are tough**: When things get tough, people who struggle with imposter syndrome can be tempted to let their fears and anxieties get the best of them. They think quitting their jobs before someone can fire them is the best way to protect themselves from being rejected or exposed as imperfect. People who get into this habit can miss amazing opportunities for growth. Worse, they give up on themselves and allow a fear of failure to stall their careers.

- **Dealing with challenging coworkers**: All of us are going to be faced with challenging coworkers. You know who I'm talking about: "idea vampires" who hear your thoughts and present them as their own. Passive-aggressive bosses. Gossipy cubemates. People who constantly interrupt you when you try to talk. It's always hard to navigate these situations, but it's part of the career journey. Building perseverance is tough when you're surrounded by conflict.

- **Baggage, aka "real life"**: Regardless of upbringing, we all can have things that happened in our past creep into our present-day lives. I recommend that we start by simply acknowledging this and giving ourselves the gift of perspective. You aren't alone in your struggles—seek help and support where you need it.

- **Living as a person of color**: Yes, we all carry bias, yet I firmly believe that hatefulness directed to any of us is an affront to us all. I stand as an ally to those of us who face disenfranchisement in the workplace. Since the murder of George Floyd in 2020, I've found myself educating my peers and colleagues on how challenging it is to be a Black person in America and in the corporate world. Black Lives Matter, period. Our pain is real, and I want everyone to see me. While more light is being shed on the harmful effect of bias and racism in the workplace, it bears noting that women of color face unique challenges in their careers. If you want to help improve diversity and inclusiveness in your sphere of influence, take time to help those who don't look like you. One of my favorite books on the topic is Minda Harts's book *The Memo*. In it, she shares her story, opens a dialogue about what women of color deal with within the workplace, and offers advice on navigating office politics, networking, and careers. I am also grateful to Minda and her encouragement for me to continue in my research agenda.

- **Neglecting self-care**: Also key to perseverance is avoiding burnout. High achievers can push themselves too fast and too hard. If you are under stress, you risk your well-being for fear of failure and inevitably hit a wall. Know how to take breaks and relax. Take your vacations—they are important for your mental health and stamina.

When You Are Ready to Quit

Several years ago, I received a frantic call from Stephanie, a rock-star former colleague.

"Candace," she said, *"I can't take it anymore! Tomorrow, I'm submitting my resignation. I know I can get another job."*

I asked her what was going on. *"My boss is impossible!"* she replied. *"For the past two months I've been doing my job, and I've taken on the responsibilities of a colleague who is out on leave. I'm killing myself, and I don't see any end in sight. I feel like I'm being taken advantage of, and it's so unfair. I'm out!"*

I could hear the frustration in her voice. She was clearly at her breaking point. I told her how sorry I was—I knew how talented she was and hated to see her so upset.

While I felt for her and wanted her to be happy, I also knew that she was the primary breadwinner in her household. I asked her whether she had a year's worth of her family's household expenses in her bank account.

Stephanie was silent for a moment. *"No,"* she admitted quietly. *"I probably have three months'."*

I reminded her that if she submitted her resignation tomorrow and started looking for work immediately, it would take three to four months at best for her to complete an interview and hiring cycle. What if that process happened several times? She was an amazing employee, but it wasn't out of the realm of possibility that she would take much longer than three months to land her next job. What would happen to her family then? I also shared that her sense of fear and uncertainty could lead to feelings of desperation that would show up in her interviews. She needed to be intentional and secure in her action plan.

Of course, Stephanie's life and choices were all her own. What I recommended for her is what I recommend to anyone who comes to me in a highly emotional state, ready to quit their role in frustration.

1. **Sit down with whomever you share finances with and have an honest talk**. Don't make any decisions that

will dramatically impact your family's life without talking it through first.

2. **Make an appointment to speak with your manager or boss.** Chances are that your boss doesn't want you to leave. Be honest about your frustrations and come armed with ideas to make it better.

3. **Manage your stress in a healthy way.** Whether it's exercise, a vacation, or a night out with friends, do what you need to do to unwind and de-stress.

Two weeks later, Stephanie called me back and said *"OK, I didn't resign. My husband and I spoke, and we have a plan in place to save money. I spoke with my boss. She thanked me for stepping up and being the person on my team she can count on to deliver. She's in a bind because she can't do anything while my colleague is on leave. She asked me to trust her."*

A few months later, Stephanie called me back. Things were unchanged in her work situation; however, the communication between her and her manager had greatly improved. There was a resolution in sight, and in thirty days she'd be receiving her bonus. Additionally, she and her husband had made some financial decisions that would free up a year's worth of income if she did decide to quit down the road.

Soon after, I received a text from Stephanie. She had just earned recognition from her company for her contributions—in front of her peers. A short time later, she sent another text: *Call me when you can. I want to tell you this news live!*

I could hear the joy in her voice when I called her back. *"I've just reached the executive ranks in my company! I am now making a salary that I had never even thought possible within the timeframe that I had in mind. Thank you so much for helping me stay there four months ago when I was ready to walk out. It was tough, but I stuck in there, and now my career is taking off in a way that I hadn't even imagined."*

Stephanie's story is a great reminder that perseverance during times of stress isn't always easy—but sometimes, it can pay off in the long run.

One of the biggest parts of perseverance is endurance. You aren't doing yourself any favors by working yourself to the ground.

This isn't to say that there won't be times when throwing yourself into work is a good idea. I remember once being "dissed and dumped." I was so brokenhearted that I poured all my frustration into my work. In four months, I made my goal for the entire year. That success helped me feel better. Working hard at the things you're good at can be great therapy sometimes.

The trick to perseverance is being grounded in your values. Are you moving toward your goals or someone else's projection of their goals onto you? Counsel and advice are important; be sure you're going after what you want, because you're the one who will put in the work and time and bear the consequences and trade-offs.

It also helps to listen to your body. Even athletes who run long distances know the importance of taking breaks when you need them. Whether that means yoga, meditation, a long vacation, or a quick phone call with a friend, pace yourself.

You'll find the long game much easier if you do.

Perseverance and Self-Efficacy

None of this is to say that your career will always be tough. It won't! The point isn't that you'll need to reach deep within yourself to persevere day in and day out. If you do find yourself in that situation, it's probably smart to step back and do some evaluating.

I want you to get to a place where, when you feel fear or discomfort, you welcome it as part of your journey. I want you to see it as a place to put your self-efficacy into action.

Much of the research around women in the workplace shows a common theme among those who quit their jobs due to stress. Many women in my research articulated that they felt that, when they'd given up on a project or quit a job in the past, they had done so too soon.

"I wish I would have stuck it out" is a sad sentiment to take with you through life. If I think back to my conversation with Beverly all those years ago, I think she would agree with you. You are creating your own amazing life story.

I want you to feel empowered to make life look exactly the way you want it to look, and I don't want fear or anxiety to get in your way.

If you find yourself suffering in silence, or if quitting when times get tough seems like a pattern for you, I leave you with this final thought:

The path toward self-efficacy is paved with perseverance.

It's incredibly important that you prioritize your well-being and mental health so your mindset allows you to believe that sticking it out is a possibility. Know your boundaries. Clarify your non-negotiables.

Get yourself a network and the tools you need for your journey.

Your Persevere Career Zone: Where are you now?

Building your perseverance muscle is a long journey, but so worth it. In the next chapter we will talk about how education can help (stay tuned).

In the meantime, I recognize that dealing with these pitfalls can be challenging, to be sure, but here are a few ways I've helped myself and others develop perseverance during hard times:

1. **Practice acceptance.** The final stage of coping with grief or loss is accepting reality for what it is. If you haven't heard the Serenity Prayer written by American theologian Reinhold Niebuhr, it goes like this: Father, give us courage to change what must be altered, serenity to accept what cannot be helped, and the insight to know one from the other. This prayer has certainly helped me persevere through hard times.

2. **Turn to music.** When I'm driving to and from work, I take the advice a friend gave me a long time ago and listen to music that will put me in the mindset I want to be in when I walk into the office or my home. I have playlists for inspiration, concentration, meditation, energy, and anything in between.

3. **Reach out for help.** I know I've said this a few times, but it's so important it bears repeating: you are not going through this alone. Find trusted friends and advisors you can turn to when work is hard.

4. **Practice self-care.** Self-care is about much more than a once-a-year spa day. Keep yourself healthy with enough sleep, relaxation, and down time; that way, when you need to keep yourself motivated, you have enough energy to do so.

5. **Consider your past.** Reflect on times you've overcome adversity. What did you do to get through it? What worked to help you feel better and to carry more energy and a better sense of purpose?

6. **Turn inward.** For some, this will mean leaning on your faith, reflection, or meditation practice. For others, it will mean going on a long walk every night before bed. Whatever this means for you, prioritize it.

7. **Get professional help.** If you own your own business or feel stuck in your career, this might mean hiring a coach or team to help you with all the facets of your work that are particularly challenging. If you need to reach out to someone on a more personal level, a therapist can be incredibly helpful.

8. **Tap into your network.** Investigate networking opportunities within your organization; or, if you own your own

business, make time to connect with and build your network regularly. These relationships will fortify you when times are difficult.

9. **Practice positive affirmations.** This really works! Wake up every day and remind yourself of how smart and capable you are. Celebrate all the ways you've overcome difficulty in the past. These small affirmations can be incredibly powerful when you're in need of support and strength.

10. **Reframe the situation.** When in doubt, look at your situation from a different point of view. Can your challenge be viewed positively in any way? Get help from others if this is difficult for you to do in the moment.

Now that you know the importance of saving for your future, working hard, and advocating for yourself, consider where you are in the section of perseverance. The colors Red, Yellow, and Green in the assessment chart are visual indicators that you are moving in the right path toward strengthening your self-efficacy and perseverance skills. As you read the next chart, consider where you are in the framework and how you can start planning to move forward from what's holding you back and celebrate your progress.

Career Zone Assessment: Persevere

Red Career Zone	Yellow Career Zone	Green Career Zone
• I tend to quit or threaten to quit whenever there is a challenge at work. • I refuse to admit failures or mistakes. • I see asking for help as a sign of weakness. • I constantly assume I am not good enough for my job. • I figure most people are out to get me. • I'd rather suffer in silence than speak up for myself. • I leave projects halfway through when they seem too hard. • I never take vacations. • I don't know how to deal with my current problem. • I am in denial about my current situation.	• I find ways to confront challenges. • I take responsibility for failures and mistakes. • I have a network of people I can rely on for guidance and help when needed. • I feel confident in my abilities most of the time. • I seek out varying opinions when I feel stuck but not defeated. • I give myself breaks when I can feel myself burning out. • I am careful not to blame myself. • I can still appreciate the positive aspects of my life, career, and journey. • I can tap into my faith and/or purpose for hope.	• I constructively confront stressful situations. • I welcome challenges as a means for my growth. • I admit mistakes and am happy to share my learning and growth with others. • I have an amazing network of people to help me through hard times, and I actively help others too. • I never doubt that, despite my mistakes, I'm an asset to my company and team. • I spend time planning vacations and have clear boundaries around downtime. • I don't get threatened by change. • I can reframe the situation. • I understand what my choice is or what is in my control. • I can prioritize my mental health and well-being as I manage this situation.

KEY CHAPTER TAKEAWAYS:

- Demonstrating perseverance, having grit, and displaying resilience help to strengthen self-efficacy.

- Your career journey will require you to weather storms. Resist the urge to immediately quit or give up when times are challenging. Reach out to others and ask for support when you need it. Be empathetic; you never know what someone has been through.

- You have more grit and resilience than you realize. Any adversity you've faced getting to this point is strength you'll call upon during any workplace challenges.

- If you own your own business, you will require an extra dose of perseverance at times. This is all the more reason to take good care of your mental health and build the endurance you'll need to weather the ups and downs of entrepreneurship.

- Getting to the Green Behaviors requires practice. Know yourself, your triggers, and the ways in which you can keep yourself calm and centered.

Questions for Further Discussion with Your Support Circle

Building perseverance is so much easier when you surround yourself with an amazing network of people and mentors who can help you see clearly. Use these questions to talk through the key points in this chapter and revisit them when you are faced with challenges along your career journey. Have a conversation, be open to new ideas and suggestions, and don't forget to download the accompanying workbook to help keep you accountable.

What She Said . . . Reflections from Women

Sometimes it can be difficult to begin a discussion on the topic of how to navigate trying or difficult situations. Below is a series of responses from the women in my study related to the concept of perseverance. Do any of these statements ring true for you? Why or why not?

- *While "Do what you love" is good advice, sometimes you don't know what you'd love to do. Takes a while to find out.*

- *An example of career advice women get that is more harmful than helpful is to just stick it out.*

- *Often women get the advice to sexualize themselves to satisfy men when in fact that will actually harm their reputation to the public.*

- *Not every woman belongs at the top of the ladder. We should all appreciate our roles and contributions, whether big or small, no matter if we're on the ladder or not.*

- *Women could be in a toxic workplace, and that could negatively impact their work.*

- *Although it might not be directly stated, there's an implication that you must act like a man to make it in a man's world. In my opinion, it's important to be yourself and rely on your ability and personal strengths.*

- *I haven't been told things blatantly, but rather been made to accept the "Good Old Boys" network in certain positions.*

Additional Questions to Consider:

- Do you know your tipping points as they pertain to work and stress? What are they?

- How do gender roles in our society impact the workplace?

- What past experiences can you draw on to help you navigate a current opportunity or dilemma?

- What are you proud of about your career journey?

- What activities or routines do you practice on a regular basis to rest, restore, and recharge yourself?

- How do you reward yourself for your accomplishments?

- What are some of the best ways to handle career disappointments?

- What positive self-talk do you share with yourself?

- How do you own and reconcile your mistakes?

- If you own your own business, how are you keeping yourself motivated and connected with others? How can you do this even better in the future?

- What do you do or who do you talk to when you are feeling anxious?

- Are you inspired or deflated by the success of others? Why?

CHAPTER 5:
EDUCATE YOURSELF ON HOW TO EXPAND YOUR SKILLS AND KNOWLEDGE THROUGHOUT YOUR CAREER

"Education helps women get into positions that others might try to disqualify them from obtaining. Education broadens perspective and helps with giving women the opportunity to build on their knowledge, skills, education, and experiences to be more effective and build confidence within themselves."

—Anna, Gen X, hotel general manager

The E in the SHAPE framework represents *Educate*. In my study, so many women expressed regret for their lack of formal education or training and how this lack blunted their careers. However, I've found that women of all generations prioritize performance, and since professional development boosts self-efficacy, being a lifelong learner can pay off well.

Committing to a strong educational foundation beyond your diploma(s) is the final step in the SHAPE method for a reason. It's because you've now gotten to a point where you realize that there are certain things you'll never be "done" with in your career journey.

You guessed it: knowledge, expertise, and additional certification and degrees. In other words, continuing education and lifelong learning.

It's easy to get to this part in the SHAPE method and panic. During my talks, I hear alarmed statements from women all the time when I mention that a commitment to lifelong education is the final, crucial step in building your self-efficacy and a long-lasting, successful career. See if any of these statements sound familiar:

- *I don't have a degree from a great college! I can't go back in time and change my undergraduate degree!*

- *I've worked my way up through this organization through experience and skill. Do I really need to go back to school and get an advanced degree?*

- *Now that I have a spouse and kids, the time has passed for me to seriously consider higher education. I guess I'll just remain stuck where I am.*

- *How do I know what degrees or certifications I need for the job I really want?*

- *The job I really want requires experience I don't have—how do I go about getting that experience?*
- *I have a degree in X, but you know what? I've always wanted to study Y. What do I do?*

If you find yourself thinking any of these topics, I want you to remember that this is where that all-important self-efficacy comes in. Committing to your lifelong development—especially if your career trajectory isn't a straight line—requires the skills we've already talked about in this book.

Commit to lifelong learning, whatever that might look like for you.

I always start by asking my audience to get "real" with who you are: your strengths, weaknesses, conversational styles, triggers, fears, and inspirations. In other words, start with a sense of curiosity about how you can improve. When you're first starting out in your career, this seems obvious. Fresh out of college, starting at a new organization as the "newbie" is scary and overwhelming. You're ready to learn as much as you can. However, as we continue in our careers, it can become easy to forget that your ultimate career success is a journey, not a destination.

I believe that education helps women a lot in the long run. It makes them strong and confident. Moreover, it makes them independent without having to rely on anyone. Finally, they can boost their self-efficacy to withstand other obstacles.

No matter how much you think you've learned, you can always learn more.

I once worked with a woman—let's call her Tracy—whose career was on an upward trajectory for more than a decade after she finished college. School had always come easily for her, and advanced certifications were like checkboxes she could complete easily. It seemed like every promotion, every accolade easily came her way.

That all stopped when she wanted to move into managing people.

Suddenly, her degrees and certificates weren't enough. She was being passed over for management roles, and she couldn't figure out why.

When we spoke, she was determined that she must be missing something. Instead of pushing her toward a skill she could list on her resume, I encouraged her to take a personality assessment online (there are many available—try the Myers-Briggs Type Indicator to start). I figured that what she would find there would enlighten her about why management roles were going to other people. I also told her to ask her current manager for honest feedback about her communication style—there might be something she wasn't aware of that she would need to change if she wanted to manage people.

At first, Tracy was shocked to discover that her very direct communication style was off-putting to others. She was quick to defend herself and her actions. She'd gotten this far, hadn't she? If other people were intimidated by her intellect, wasn't that their problem?

The truth was this simple personality test was more of an education for this woman than any advanced degree could have given her. She realized that if she wanted to manage others, she would have to be more aware of how they perceived her.

This is what I mean by getting curious about how you can improve. It's a mindset that will help you weather ups and downs as well as make informed decisions about your future.

An Educational Foundation

If you've gotten this far in the book, I'm hoping it's obvious that what you learn in high school, college, and beyond isn't all you need to know in order to have a successful career. In fact, you could have all the degrees in the world from the most prestigious universities and still struggle with managing money, advocating for yourself and your career, and persevering through hard times.

When I talk about creating a strong educational foundation, I'm not just talking about accumulating great test results, degrees, and accolades. Don't get me wrong—that type of education is important!

What I'm talking about here is a lifelong commitment to your development and learning.

"Education is a key factor. If we are educated, we develop the confidence to shine. If we know what we are talking about, then we have all the tools to do the job."

—Helen, Gen X, project manager

In my TEDx Talk, I advise women to commit to keeping their skills and knowledge current so that they will feel equipped to succeed when they want to advance.

For some, this will mean continual, ongoing certification. For others, it may mean practicing something new on your job or maybe earning certification in an area of study you haven't explored before. For all of us, it will mean putting our ongoing development at the top of our priority lists, for the lifetime of our careers.

As with all things, making your continual education a priority will take practice. We're all juggling a lot, burning the candle at both ends, and trying to balance work and home life while keeping our sanity. I get it!

But what I'm here to tell you is that even though it can seem overwhelming to take time to further your development, the skills you develop there will benefit you greatly in the long run—whether it be through a night class or an additional credential or a coaching program.

Don't believe me? By having a strong educational foundation, you build your self-efficacy. When you're performing your role or managing your business, you feel confident that you have what you need to do well. When you want to advance or expand, you feel better prepared to take that next step.

In other words, your continued professional development is at the core of the SHAPE method.

Education and How Women Lead

Recent decades have revealed the influence of a woman's education, both formal and informal, on how she leads. While there is a tendency to link formal education to success, the data tell us a different story. Here are a couple interesting things to keep in mind as you apply the Education portion of the SHAPE method to your career:

- **There is no one set of instructions for how women become leaders.** Most frequently, women's leadership is described through factors such as self-awareness, courage, resilience, and collaboration.[39,40] Both Woollen (2016)[41] and Isaac (2007)[42] describe leadership as "multidimensional."

- **It is important to consider conditions that impact women's access to leadership positions beyond individual characteristics.** Research found that traditionally male-dominated leadership culture poses challenges for women seeking senior positions.[43] In other words, our culture and circumstances matter, especially for women in leadership.

So yes, education is important. But education goes far beyond the classroom. The data show us that what makes effective leaders is often the "soft skills" that come from life experience and resilience.

The good news is that you have control over this. Part of taking ownership of your career means taking an honest look at your strengths and weaknesses and getting serious about improving in areas where you struggle.

---

39 Isaac, C. (2007). *Women deans: Patterns of power.* University Press of America.

40 Madsen, S. R. (2008). *On becoming a woman leader: Learning from the experiences of university presidents.* John Wiley & Sons.

41 Woollen, S. (2016). The road less traveled: Career trajectories of six women presidents in higher education. *Advancing Women in Leadership, 36,* 1–10.

42 Isaac, C. (2007). *Women deans: Patterns of power.* University Press of America.

43 Ford, D. S. (2014). Rising to the top: Career progression of women senior-level student affairs administrators [Doctoral dissertation]. ProQuest.

You may be a person who "hates" school. I can't tell you how many times I hear this phrase from the most talented and brilliant women. There are many ways to increase your knowledge base without a formal education, yet in many organizations you may face tradeoffs related to lack of compensation and advancement without a formal education. And there are many, many ways to advance your professional development, as we'll discuss in this chapter.

Professional Development in Practice

Many organizations will offer employees a wide variety of professional development opportunities, some of which will be amazingly impactful for your careers, and others not so much. No matter if you're just starting in your career or are close to retirement, professional development will likely be an expectation and a requirement.

In 2018, Jennifer Wegner published "Lessons from Women Leaders: The Impact of Professional Development.[44]" Her findings around professional development experiences and their impact on women's career ascension are truly fascinating. She focused on professional development, what it means for women in the workplace, and how it can be best implemented. What she determined centered on motivation and gained knowledge.

First, we need to feel motivated to learn the material. Second, we need to feel like we can take what we've learned and apply it in a meaningful way.

This is important information for managers who are organizing formal professional development, but it's also important for us as individuals to understand as we take ownership of our own career paths.

Here's where self-efficacy comes in yet again. You understand how important professional development is, but that doesn't mean every opportunity is one you should take. Before you commit to a week-long conference, a coaching program, an advanced degree, or anything else

---

44 Wegner, J. (2018). Lessons from women leaders: The impact of professional development. *The Vermont Connection, 39*(15). https://scholarworks.uvm.edu/tvc/vol39/iss1/15

that will take your time, energy, and commitment, you should have the confidence to jump forward eagerly or politely pass.

Based on Wegner's research, you should be asking the following questions:

- Can I enthusiastically commit to learning this material?

- Will this content help me specialize or become more specialized in my field?

- Will this professional development help me connect more deeply with my colleagues?

Again, all the confidence you've built in the SHAPE method is crucial in these situations. When it comes to committing to long-term education and growth, you're going to have to consider your finances as well as your goals for life and work. Continuing education, training, and professional development are crucial. Remember, you want to be judicious with your money, time, and energy too.

Professional Development as a Business Owner

Being a business owner presents its own unique rewards and challenges, and this is certainly no different when it comes to continuing education. The good news is that when you are in the driver's seat of your company, you get to decide what the "must-haves" are in terms of certifications.

The bad news is that if you are not careful, you might be tempted to let yourself get inundated with the day-to-day work of owning and operating the business. Your continuing education might go so far to the back burner that it's forgotten for months or even years.

I once worked with a woman who had built a thriving business as a nutritionist. She'd been so busy for so many years that it never occurred to her that she might want to pursue a degree beyond her bachelor's degree in nutrition. Then, her dream job opened in a hospital she really wanted to work for. Her resume spoke for itself, and she nailed the interview. But she didn't get the job.

The recruiter called her to tell her what an outstanding candidate she was, but they'd simply had to go with another candidate. "She had a master's degree," the recruiter told her. "If you'd had a master's, the job would have been yours."

It's hard to believe that the lack of a degree holds someone with experience back. But it still happens. And my colleague was devastated.

The truth is that many professionals, especially business owners, will have careers that span multiple decades. During this time, it is wise to be prepared for new types of jobs, new technologies, and new problems that do not yet exist. Of course, this highlights the need for innovative forms of continuing education and professional development that allow women to be ahead of the curve in terms of leadership strategies, human resource development, and technological knowledge.[45]

In my experience, female business owners who have spent time on the previous steps of the SHAPE method are in a much better position to form a plan for their ongoing education. This is because they have already developed the self-efficacy to look impartially at their business and goals and be realistic about what they can expect in keeping themselves at the top of their game.

Here are some questions that will help you develop a plan for ongoing education if you are a business owner:

1. What sorts of degrees or certifications do other entrepreneurs in my field have?

2. Is there a specific job that I want five, ten, even fifteen years down the road? Would an additional degree help me make that dream job happen?

3. How might additional certification be an asset as I provide value to my customers?

---

45 Darling-Hammond, L., Barron, B., Pearson, P. D., Schoenfeld, A. H., Stage, E. K., Zimmerman, T. D., Cervetti, G. N., & Tilson, J. L. (2008). *Powerful learning: What we know about teaching for understanding.* Jossey-Bass.

4. What partnerships can I create that might provide ongoing education for myself and my team outside the "classroom" experience?

The good news is that it is never too late to pursue the knowledge you need to continue to grow as a business owner. Opportunities that are lost are in the past, and there will always be more in the future.

Meaning and Motivation: Focus on Your Professional Development

We already know that female leaders are successful due to their commitment to self-awareness, their courage in the workplace and beyond, their resilience and perseverance, and their willingness to collaborate with others.[46,47] According to Isaac's and Woollen's research, successful female leaders are "multidimensional" in a way that is different from their male counterparts. There are simply more conditions that impact a woman's success in the workplace. You're probably reading this and nodding your head in agreement. I know I was when I encountered this research!

What does this mean for you? Well, because of our "multidimensional" (aka complicated) life circumstances, women will have more challenges seeking senior positions in male-dominated fields. All this is to say that this final piece of the SHAPE method is especially critical for women. It means that the professional development you commit to will inform the entire trajectory of your career.

Professional development, whether it's in the classroom, on the job, or in any other capacity, will require two things of you: meaning and motivation.

In her 2018 study, Wegner discovered that what participants identify they gained from professional development is, in large part,

---

46 Isaac, C. (2007). *Women deans: Patterns of power.* University Press of America.

47 Madsen, S. R. (2008). *On becoming a woman leader: Learning from the experiences of university presidents.* John Wiley & Sons.

informed by their motivation to both understand the impact of the experience and make it meaningful.

Simply put, the most successful women don't learn things to check off a box. They learn things that they know have meaning to their career, their impact, and their future success.

Undoubtedly, some learning experiences you will need to take part in will feel like a drag. I never said committing to your lifelong education would always be a walk in the park!

What I will say is that the self-efficacy you've practiced thus far in the SHAPE method will set you up to approach your lifelong learning by leading with meaning, motivation, and intentionality.

- If you aren't sure what the "point" of learning a certain skill is, ask your boss or mentor.

- If you manage people, be sure not to throw opportunities at them without being clear on why you're having them do it.

- If your motivation is lacking, be honest with yourself about what you need to persevere. Have conversations with others, allowing yourself to be vulnerable and open to suggestions and feedback.

- If you want to go back to school but you're short on funds, figure out a way to get your employer to pay for your continued professional development. Many organizations offer this, and it never hurts to ask!

The points above highlight what I mean when I say education is a commitment. The self-efficacy skills you've learned up to this point will make the difference between career satisfaction or simply going through the motions.

Women and Opportunities for Further Education

What we know from the research is clear: when women feel like their continued education, whatever that looks like, is valuable, it will help to build not only their resume but also their self-efficacy.

Thankfully, as workspaces grow increasingly diverse, we see leaders around the world rethinking how they value employees in terms of education and experience. This is great news for people who simply cannot afford the degree they have always dreamed of, as well as business owners who need more flexible ways to stay at the top of their game while meeting their day-to-day demands.

So take heart as you embark on this last, never-ending path of your SHAPE program. Your continual education is an investment in your work *and* your well-being. Be curious and take advantage of all opportunities you can that will fill you with purpose!

Your Education Career Zone: Where are you now?

Getting into the Green Career Zone Behaviors when it comes to education is a lifelong effort. Fortunately, there are many ways you can work toward your continuing education that do not require a huge time or financial commitment. Here are some of my favorites:

- **Start with you.** Start with an assessment, such as the Myers-Briggs or the Enneagram. The results might be very valuable for you as you figure out how you show up the best, how you learn, and what you value in terms of development.

- **Ask those who know you best.** Consider asking your family, close friends, or peers questions about your strengths, areas for development, or advice.

- **Tap into free resources.** Subscribe to podcasts that will help you grow in your knowledge of your craft or business. Sure, you won't get a degree from completing them, but you will undoubtedly be able to speak to trends and make informed decisions about your work as a result.

- **Look beyond universities.** Seek out opportunities for

weekend or online classes through your community education department. These are often very cost effective and will help you network with other people in your line of work.

- **Seek out events.** Attend speaking events hosted by people you admire. Oftentimes these are free or low cost, and you will leave with a wealth of knowledge and encouragement.

- **Speak with mentors.** Who are some of the people in your field whom you admire? Can you buy them coffee and ask them about their educational path and suggestions for people who want to do what they do?

- **Business owners, create learning opportunities for your team.** Can you invite a guest speaker to a staff meeting? Can you offer tuition assistance if your team seeks out higher education?

- **Model lifelong learning.** This is especially important if you own your own business. Show your staff and clients that you value education by constantly learning yourself.

- **Be curious.** Learning begins with curiosity. Let go of big expectations and start here. What are you most curious about in your field, and how can you learn more about it?

- **Curate your experience on social media.** LinkedIn, for example, has a library of courses for business professionals. If you are on social media, don't let it be a time suck—use it to your advantage and learn on those platforms through videos and professional groups.

- **Read, read, read!** You have time to read, I promise you. Visit your local library or bookstore, download audiobooks for when you walk the dog, or whatever else works for your schedule. Make reading a daily and lifelong habit.

As a reminder, the colors Red, Yellow, and Green listed in the next chart are visual indicators that you are building a mindset to position yourself for the career you want and deserve. As you read the next chart, consider where you are on the path to lifelong learning and development and how you can start planning to move forward from what's holding you back and celebrate your progress.

Career Zone Assessment: Education

Red Career Zone	Yellow Career Zone	Green Career Zone
• I display a generally negative attitude toward learning new things. • I constantly feel like I am the "smartest person in the room" and that no one can teach me anything. • I want to pursue advanced education, but give up when it feels too hard. • I don't have a plan to pay for education. • I have too much debt to go back to school. • I don't have a support system. • I don't believe I can be successful in school. • I hated high school, college, and learning new things. • I like to tease people for attaining knowledge. • I don't have or can't make time to learn a new skill or earn a degree.	• I am working on my professional development. • I am happy to learn from others on my team or in my organization. • I actively seek out professional development opportunities. • I display a positive attitude toward further learning. • I understand how I can fund my training and development. • I want to pursue a management role, but I don't like math and am taking steps to improve my business knowledge. • I can manage my time to make room for more training and development. • I have a support system. • I understand my options and the trade-offs I need to make to enhance my development. • I am in an environment where professional development is encouraged.	• I constantly seek out advice and opportunities for growth. • I find a way to make further development a priority in my life. • I am constantly open to learning from others. • I display a positive attitude toward further learning and encourage others to do the same. • I speak up when I have questions about learning opportunities I'm presented with. • I actively support and coach others in their professional development journey. • I am determined to keep trying in spite of a setback. • I am not afraid to invest in my growth. • I make time to learn new things. • I will seek help along my journey to keep me going.

KEY CHAPTER TAKEAWAYS:

- Knowing what educational opportunities to pursue and take advantage of throughout your career will require the self-efficacy skills you've worked toward. As always, that's the key!

- Your commitment to lifelong education is crucial to your success in the long term.

- "Education" is more than just degrees or checked boxes. Actively seek out ways to build your leadership skillset, both personally and professionally.

- If you are a business owner, pay careful attention to cultivating your continued education as well as opportunities for your team.

- All you've learned up to this point is crucial for keeping yourself in an educational mindset. Ask for help, guidance, and support where you need it!

Questions for Further Discussion with Your Support Circle

Having a group of people to whom you are accountable for continuing education can be incredibly valuable. Use these questions to help you navigate your educational opportunities and questions throughout your career. Have a conversation, be open to new ideas and suggestions, and don't forget to download the accompanying workbook to help keep you accountable.

What She Said . . . Reflections from Women

Sometimes it can be difficult to begin a discussion about advancing your education, training, or professional development. Below is a series of responses from the women in my study related to the concepts of enhancing your knowledge, training, and education. Do any of these statements ring true for you? Why or why not?

- *A good education is important, yet being willing to work hard is more important.*

- *I think being well educated helps women get a better footing, but I still think there are many barriers we need to overcome. Sometimes it's just the difference in dispositions compared to male colleagues; other times it's just getting the negative "labels" and stereotypes removed. Plus, not being "too nice" or being afraid to say no or take charge.*

- *I think anytime you educate yourself, it's another level of confidence. Women deserve to do things for themselves, and education is a powerful tool.*

- *I think education plays a significant role in women's success; however, I do not believe that education is necessary to succeed. I believe if you work hard and use your intelligence and resources, you will succeed.*

- *Education helps a woman with independence and self-esteem. It makes her a better wife, mother, and employee.*

- *I hated school! Do I really need to go back?*

- *I have my GED and believe I can get more jobs as a result.*

- *It depends on the situation. Some women can achieve success without an education.*

- *Women are already viewed as incapable or lesser than. Achieving a high education allows for credentials and networking. In doing so, women use the same system used by their counterparts to get where they would like to be. Education also enables the use of resources and strengthens skills like critical thinking and problem-solving.*

- *The training to help women get ahead in the world is the first best option to help them understand their career options.*

Additional Questions to Consider:

- Do you believe you need more education and training at this phase of your career? Why or why not?

- What are some of the ways you've expanded your knowledge base using formal education?

- What are some of the ways you've expanded your knowledge base outside of formal education?

- Have you found any assessment tools particularly helpful?

- How do you learn best?

- Does your employer provide professional development or tuition reimbursement assistance? If so, can you take advantage of it to meet your education goals?

- Does your employer provide resources for additional learning? Are you taking advantage of those?

- If you are a business owner, do you provide opportunities for additional learning for your employees?

- If you are self-employed, how can you make lifelong learning a part of your life?

- What free resources do you use that help you with your day-to-day activities?

- What skills do you wish you could acquire in your field?

- Do you participate in industry or trade associations? If not, why not?

- Do you know the certifications that are relevant for your field? Do you have plans to pursue them?

WHERE TO GO FROM HERE

"I was never given ANY type of career advice."

—Rachel, baby boomer, finance director

"I wish I'd had advice before I started my business. I was on my own."

—Tonya, Gen X, business owner

"Women are always told to listen, and listening is a good thing, but men are told to do the opposite. Women should be told to speak up and share their ideas, because women in these fields are just as capable as men."

—Jill, millennial, communications director

If I could go back in time and talk to myself as I was first starting out in my career, I would tell myself one very simple thing: everything will be all right.

Every setback. Every disappointment. Every decision I made without knowing if it was "right" or "wrong." All of it would turn out all right.

This might be easy for me to say now, but keep in mind that I wasn't always at the top of my game. At first, it was a lonely journey. I knew what I wanted, but I would lie awake at night trying to figure out how to make it work. I didn't fear failure, but I did worry that if I fell, I wouldn't know how to pick myself back up and keep going. I felt constant pressure, especially as a Black woman, to excel and live up to everyone's expectations. There was much I didn't realize about the choices I made, the trade-offs I would have to make, and the confidence I would need to rely on when things felt uncertain.

I wish I would have known then that I didn't have to do any of this on my own. I could reach out for help. I could reach down to help others. The journey is hard enough—don't do it alone.

The tools and research I've shared with you in this book are not meant to be a checklist completed in chronological order. You are in the best position to know when is the "right" time for you to go for a promotion or step away from your career for a while. The truth is that putting this method into practice means your mindset will shift. You'll commit to saving to create a strong financial future for yourself and benefit from the peace of mind to pursue something new. As the difficulty of your work ebbs and flows, you'll create habits around advocating for yourself and persevering to keep you on track or help you to pivot. You'll never stop educating yourself and improving upon your skillset, which will strengthen how you feel about being successful if you step outside you comfort zone.

In other words, the SHAPE method is fluid and will look like this as you mature and grow in your own career:

S: SAVE

Save for the future you want. Make it a daily, weekly, monthly, and yearly habit to be on top of your finances. You will never want to lose focus of this, no matter how your salary might fluctuate over the years.

H: HARD WORK

Working hard means more than just putting in hours. It always means taking steps to understand what's expected of you and making sure you are meeting the expectations of key decision-makers. This is true when you start out and will be true through your entire career.

A: ADVOCATE

Speaking up for what you feel and deserve isn't something you can do once or twice and never worry about again. Advocacy, especially for women, is a crucial life skill that will be easier the more you practice and gain confidence.

P: PERSEVERE

Will there be tough times? Absolutely. Challenges aren't just reserved for when you start out. You can be certain that your entire career will be filled with ups, downs, and plenty of moments where you will want to quit. Learn perseverance skills to take with you for the long haul.

E: EDUCATE

A dedication to lifelong education is essential for you as you build and undertake your career journey. At some points, that step might look like earning an additional certification or degree. At others, it might mean more focus on mentorships and work experience. No matter what, you will want to make committing to further education a priority until the day you decide to retire.

In the introduction, I mentioned that my fascination with both generational differences and the role women play in the workforce informed my doctoral studies and laid the foundation for this book. Even after all that education and work, I *still* faced challenges getting people to see past the tired narratives that women were holding themselves back.

Start by being conscious of these self-destructive narratives and focus on a new narrative for yourself as you move forward.

Use the templates I've provided. Head over to my website for a workbook to help keep you accountable. **But most importantly, embrace who you are as you navigate your own journey.**

I hope that this book has imparted the courage you need to step beyond any limitations you've felt when it comes to your career. I hope you'll keep it as a reference and reminder for when things feel difficult. I hope you'll show it to your friends who are just starting out on their journeys, take part in discussions about the tools, and feel empowered to figure out how to create the life and career that work for you.

I often say that I am unapologetic about using my time, talent, and resources to make the world a better place. I remind my mentees, particularly those of us who are women and people of color, to never forget to use the power of our position, influence, and purpose to look out for those who are coming up alongside and behind us. We have a responsibility to make things right and better for them, because if we don't, in all likelihood no one else will.

Remember, there are those who are looking at you for inspiration. Don't miss out on the opportunity to use the power of your influence and your purpose, no matter your role or position, to help others get to the next phase along their journey.

About the Study

The book you just read is based on the findings of a two-part qualitative and quantitative study that was conducted in the fall of 2019 and winter of 2021 to identify how women could better self-manage their career advancement. The goal of the research was to provide practical advice to female professionals as they navigate their careers and to serve as a resource for managers, mentors, and professional development professionals. I wanted to explore the factors that help women address impediments to self-efficacy to set themselves up for success in their careers.

For part one of the studies, I asked approximately 1,100 female US citizens born between 1946 and 1998 a series of thirty-seven multiple choice questions. The respondents were asked to select the best answer, rank a series of concepts, or write in a response to certain questions. The core concepts I wanted to explore were:

- What steps can women take to create a stronger foundation from which to advance their careers?

- Given what you have learned so far in your career, what advice would you give to a younger woman just starting out in her career?

Five themes emerged that served as the basis for the framework:

1. Saving: Creating a strong financial foundation

2. Hard Work: Putting in the time, energy, and effort

3. Advocacy: Putting your self-advocacy skills to practice

4. Perseverance: Building the "muscle" you need to get through challenging times

5. Education: Committing to lifelong learning, whatever that means for you

For part two of the qualitative and quantitative study, I asked 400 female US citizens born between 1946 and 1998 a series of twenty multiple choice questions in which the respondents were asked to select the best answer or write in a response to certain questions. The core concepts I wanted to explore were:

- How had their careers been affected by the five themes with the SHAPE framework?

- How had the COVID-19 pandemic impacted their career outlook?

- What advice had been more harmful than helpful to their careers?

I also included findings from my study of 1,400 female US citizens born between 1946 and 1998 on a list of twelve interpersonal communications traits described by Owen Hargie, a global scholar on communications.

The names of the participants, occupations, characteristics, and certain people in this book were anonymized using pseudonyms. The findings from the second study and my study on interpersonal communications informed the development of the Getting into the Red, Yellow, and Green Career Zone Behaviors assessment charts, the discussion guide, and the workbook for my discussion on generational communications.

APPENDIX 1:
SELF-EFFICACY ASSESSMENT

Self-efficacy is crucial to making smart decisions for your own career journey as well as keeping you focused on your goals. To understand where you are in your self-efficacy journey, ask yourself the questions below. If you believe your responses may be holding you back, this book is for you.

- **Am I stuck?** For example, when faced with a tough assignment, you can't see your way through or ask for help. You spin wheels and stress out until the house of cards you've built comes crashing down on you.

- **Do I get my feelings hurt easily?** For example, if someone disagrees with you, you shut down or withdraw without stating your case, even though everything inside tells you that you are right.

- **Do I get easily overwhelmed and freeze or give up?** For example, you become easily distracted from achieving your goals or dreams because someone criticizes you or throws a past defeat in your face.

- **Do I become paralyzed when life throws me curve-balls?** For example, you can't or won't come up with a plan B or bounce back when unexpected life events get in the way of your plans. You stay in a bad or less than ideal job, relationship, or marriage because it is easier than dealing with the situation at hand.

- **Do I live in fear?** For example, you are so scared of failure that you don't even try to apply for a promotion or a new job, even though you have a solid education and/or excellent track record of success.

- **Do I remain silent?** For example, you do nothing about your exhausting frustrations—being marginalized, ignored, and dumped on—except complain to those who can't help you. Or, you listen to their sound advice and choose not to follow it because complaining is easier.

- **Do I struggle to show any sign of leadership?** For example, you can't cope during a crisis at work, get caught up in drama, and can't keep yourself steady in tough situations. No one looks to you for strength.

- **Do I find it difficult to be flexible?** For example, you only have one go-to method of problem-solving, and when that fails, you can't find a solution. Worse, your pride won't let you ask for help or admit a mistake. You feel trapped.

- **Do I give off the impression of being inadequate?** For example, you genuinely believe that you are fragile. You have a voice in your head telling you you're not good enough, so you can't save or help yourself when faced with opportunities or challenges.

- **Do I fear change?** For example, you haven't quite reached your goal(s) within your timeframe, so you don't dare tempt fate by pursuing a new opportunity that may in fact be better than the artificial timeline you created for yourself.

Adapted from Schwarzer, R., & Jerusalem, M. (1995). Generalized self-efficacy scale. In J. Weinman, S. Wright, and M. Johnston (Eds.), Measures in health psychology: A user's portfolio. Causal and control beliefs *(35-37). Windsor, UK: NFER-Nelson.*

Schwarzer, R., & Jerusalem, M. (2004). General self-efficacy scale. In S. Salek (Ed.), Compendium of quality of life instruments, *6(2A:1). Centre for Socioeconomic Research, Cardiff University; Euromed Communications. [CD-ROM publication, without page numbers].*

APPENDIX 2:
SHAPE ACTION TEMPLATE

This SHAPE template was created to provide a general approach to adapting the framework to your circumstances.

1. **Decide which aspect(s) of the SHAPE framework you want to focus on.**

   S – Save: Create and nurture a strong financial future for yourself.

   H – Hard Work: Gain alignment with your boss on your impact.

   A – Advocate for Yourself: Put yourself out there, speak up, and get noticed.

   P – Persevere: Keep going, keep trying, and know when it's time to leave.

   E – Educate: Continually teach yourself and improve upon your skillset(s).

2. **Decide which career zone you most closely identify with currently or want to work on.**

   Where are you in your career? What career zone are you in now? Which section do you want to achieve next?

Red, Yellow, and Green
Career Zone Behaviors Defined

I use the colors Red, Yellow, and Green as markers for the SHAPE framework.

Red Zone	Yellow Zone	Green Zone
If you are in the Red career zone, you're just beginning. You are still coming to terms with what it means to be your own advocate in your career and just starting to map out a plan.	If you are in the Yellow career zone, you are taking strides toward the career you want and deserve.	If you are in the Green career zone, you are in the consistent habit of applying the SHAPE method to your career journey.
You may think: *I'm overwhelmed,* or *I can't do this.*	You may think: *I can do this,* or *I will do this.*	You may think: *I got this,* or *I am well on my way there.*
Your friends may say to you: *Come on?! You need to do this.*	Your friends may say to you: *You got this!*	Your friends may say to you: *You go!*

3. **Commit to getting into your next career zone within six months to a year.** Get started by selecting at least three items on the current section you want to achieve in the next thirty days. Reassess and increase the items on your list as needed, until you have completed or advanced into the next section. List your progress below.

What timeframe is best for you to get to the next career zone?

_____

_____

_____

_____

_____

What items in your current or the next section do you need to work on, and why?

_____

_____

_____

_____

_____

What date(s) will you plan to check on your progress?

_____

_____

_____

_____

_____

4. **Begin the discussion about your goals.**
   Speak with your partner/spouse about your plans.

When will you have the initial discussion? What questions will you ask? What are your personal and professional priorities? What are the trade-offs you need to make? What is working well? What needs to be reconsidered?

_____

_____

_____

_____

_____

What date(s) will you plan to check on your progress?

_____

_____

_____

_____

5. **Find an accountability partner such as a friend or family member to help guide you.**
   Find someone you trust and consider a financial role model to help you plan and stay on track. Discuss your goals and seek advice and support on ways to achieve them.

When will you have the initial discussion with your accountability partner? What are your immediate (e.g., one to three months), nearer-term (e.g., three months to a year), and longer-term (e.g., one to ten years) goals and retirement goals? What resources do you need? What questions do you have? What is on your bucket list?

_____

_____

_____

_____

_____

What date(s) will you plan to check on your progress?

_____

_____

_____

_____

_____

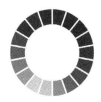

GETTING THE MOST OUT OF YOUR SUPPORT CIRCLE

When I wrote this book, I did so with the hope that readers would want to discuss its tools, research, and methods with others. Support circles are a great way to discuss your ideas and experiences, as well as bounce ideas off other professionals and get some excellent career advice for your future!

If you are new to starting a support circle, here are a few tips to get you started:

1. Start with a small number of women you trust.

2. The structure of your support circle can take many forms. For example, the group you form or join could be included as part of another group such as a reading group, employee resource group, online forum, coffee, lunch, dinner, or topical meet-up, etc.

3. Use the Key Takeaways, What She Said quotes and Additional Questions to Consider sections at the end of each chapter to help facilitate your discussions.

4. Don't be limited by the questions I ask at the end of each chapter—feel free to bring your own questions to the group.

5. Use the SHAPE ACTION TEMPLATE in Appendix 2 to keep group members thoughtful and accountable.

6. Keep the discussions confidential. Period.

A Note about Support Circles:

Don't forget that discussing the information in this book might make certain members involved in the conversation feel vulnerable or overwhelmed. This isn't your average book club—some of the things I'm asking you to think about can bring a lot of intense emotions to the surface! Do what you need to do to build trust, maintain privacy, and encourage a lively, respectful discussion, always.

For much more to help you lead discussions and to join in the conversation, I invite you to follow me on social media and visit my website, www.candacesteeleflippin.com.

ABOUT THE AUTHOR

Recognized as one of the most influential Black executives in corporate America by *Savoy Magazine*, Dr. Candace Steele Flippin is a global communications expert, multigenerational workplace scholar, TEDx speaker, and bestselling author. She is the publisher of WorkStats™ and author of *Generation Z in the Workplace* and *Millennials in the Workplace.*

Since 2016, Dr. Candace Steele Flippin has been appointed as an engaged scholar in the Weatherhead School of Management community at Case Western Reserve University. Her research focuses on practical methods to accelerate the leadership development of women, Gen X, Gen Z, and millennials in the workplace.

Dr. Candace Steele Flippin, affectionately known as "Dr. Candace," is a frequent speaker and thought leader who uses her unique background as a researcher and executive to provide practical career insights on the future of the multigenerational workplace. Her advice and research findings have been featured in *Forbes*, CNBC, CBS, *Authority Magazine*, *The Network Journal*, and Today.com. In her downtime, she collects works from emerging visual artists and enjoys traveling with her family. She and her husband live in Atlanta, Georgia. For more workplace resources, visit www.candacesteeleflippin.com.

Previous books by Dr. Candace Steele Flippin:
Generation Z in the Workplace
Millennials in the Workplace